The Regulation of Financial Markets

The Regulation of Financial Markets

PHILIP BOOTH, TIM CONGDON,
ANDREW CROCKETT, HOWARD
DAVIES, ALEXANDRE LAMFALUSSY,
WARWICK LIGHTFOOT, ADAM RIDLEY,
GEOFFREY WOOD

EDITED BY PHILIP BOOTH & DAVID CURRIE

In association with

The Institute of Economic Affairs

First published in Great Britain in 2003 by
The Institute of Economic Affairs
2 Lord North Street
Westminster
London sw1p 3lb
in association with Profile Books Ltd

The mission of the Institute of Economic Affairs is to improve public
understanding of the fundamental institutions of a free society, with
particular reference to the role of markets in solving economic and
social problems.

A CIP catalogue record for this book is available from the British Library.

ISBN 0 255 36551 9

Many IEA publications are translated into languages other than English or
are reprinted. Permission to translate or to reprint should be sought from the
Director General at the address above.

Typeset in Stone by MacGuru Ltd
info@macguru.org.uk

Printed and bound in Great Britain by Hobbs the Printers

CONTENTS

THE AUTHORS

David Currie

Since September 2002, David Currie has been chairman of OFCOM. He has been Dean of the Sir John Cass Business School (formerly known as City University Business School) since January 2001, and also Professor of Business Economics. He was formerly Professor of Economics (1988–2000) and Deputy Dean (1992–95, 1999–2000) at the London Business School, Director of the Centre of Economic Forecasting (1988–95) and Director of the Regulation Initiative at the London Business School and holder of the Sir James Ball Chair in Regulation. A well-known figure in international economic policy, David Currie has held visiting appointments at the International Monetary Fund, the Bank of England, the European University Institute and the University of Manchester. He has previously served on the Gas and Electricity Markets Authority (Ofgem, the UK energy regulator) and on the board of Abbey National, as well as on a variety of UK government advisory bodies, including the Treasury's Panel of Independent Forecasters (the 'Wise Men') and the Retail Price Index Advisory Committee. David Currie sits on the cross-benches in the House of Lords as Lord Currie of Marylebone.

Philip Booth

Philip Booth is Editorial and Programme Director at the Institute of Economic Affairs and Professor of Insurance and Risk Management at the Cass Business School, City University. Before taking up his appointment at the Institute of Economic Affairs, he was Associate Dean of the Cass Business School. Philip Booth has worked as a special adviser to the Bank of England (1998–2002). He is widely published in the fields of risk management, pensions and investment. He is co-author of the books *Modern Actuarial Theory and Practice* and *Investment Mathematics*. Philip Booth is a Fellow of the Institute of Actuaries and of the Royal Statistical Society and an Honorary Member of the Polish Society of Actuaries.

Tim Congdon

Professor Tim Congdon is one of Britain's leading economic commentators. He was a member of the Treasury's Panel of Independent Forecasters, which advised the Chancellor of the Exchequer on economic policy, between 1992 and 1997. (The Treasury Panel was similar to the President's Council of Economic Advisers in the USA.) He founded Lombard Street Research, the economic research and forecasting consultancy, in 1989, and is currently its Chief Economist. He is a research professor at Cardiff Business School and a visiting professor at the Cass Business School. He writes widely in the financial press, and makes frequent radio and television appearances.

Andrew Crockett

Andrew Crockett was general manager of the Bank for International Settlements from 1 January 1994 until 31 March 2003, and has been chairman of the Financial Stability Forum since April 1999. From 1972 to 1989 he was a staff member of the International Monetary Fund, and from 1989 to 1993 an executive director of the Bank of England. In the latter capacity, he was a member of the Monetary Committee of the European Union, Alternate Governor of the International Monetary fund for the United Kingdom, and a member (subsequently chairman) of Working Party 3 of the OECD. He is a member of the Group of Thirty and of the Board of Trustees of the International Accounting Standards Board.

Howard Davies

Howard Davies has been chairman of the Financial Services Authority since 1997. In May of that year he was asked to establish a single regulator for the UK's financial sector, merging nine separate organisations into one. In that role he represents the UK on the G7 Financial Stability Forum, the International Organisation of Securities Commissions and other international bodies.

From 1995 to 1997 he was Deputy Governor of the Bank of England. Before that, from 1992 to 1995, he was Director General of the Confederation of British Industry and, from 1987 to 1992, Controller of the Audit Commission. He was also, for six years, a director of GKN plc and a member of the International Advisory Board of NatWest.

In his earlier career he worked in the Foreign and Commonwealth Office and HM Treasury, both as an official and as special adviser to the Chancellor of the Exchequer. And for five years he worked as a management consultant for McKinsey and Company.

Alexandre Lamfalussy

Alexandre Lamfalussy served as an executive director of Banque Bruxelles Lambert and later as chairman of the executive board. In 1976 he joined the Bank for International Settlements (BIS) in Basel as Economic Adviser and Head of the Monetary and Economic Department. Between 1981 and 1985 he served as assistant general manager of the BIS before being appointed general manager in May 1985. He held this post until the end of 1993. From January 1994 until June 1997, Mr Lamfalussy was President of the European Monetary Institute in Frankfurt.

Since 1997 he has been teaching and undertaking research at the Institut d'études européennes of the Catholic University of Louvain in Louvain-la-Neuve. In August 2000 he published *Financial Crises in Emerging Markets – an essay on financial globalisation and fragility* (Yale University Press). He was chairman of the Committee of Wise Men on the Regulation of European Securities Markets set up by the European Council. The committee released its first report on 9 November 2000 and its final report on 15 February 2001. The recommendations of the committee are now being implemented.

Warwick Lightfoot

Warwick Lightfoot is an economist with interests in monetary economics, public finance and labour markets. He has been a special adviser to the Department of Employment and HM Treasury.

His articles have appeared in *The Wall Street Journal* and specialist journals ranging from the *TLS* to the *Journal of Insolvency Practitioners*.

Adam Ridley

Sir Adam Ridley trained as an economist at Oxford University and then entered the Government Economic Service, where he worked from 1965 to 1975. He advised the Conservative front bench and Research Department from 1975 to 1979 and was special adviser to the Treasury from 1979 to 1984. Sir Adam was executive director of Hambros from 1985 to 1997 and chaired the Lloyd's Names Committee 1995–96. He has been an Equitas trustee since 1996 and Director General of LIBA since 2000.

Geoffrey E. Wood

Geoffrey Wood is Professor of Economics at the Cass Business School, City University. He has also taught at the University of Warwick, and been on the research staff of the Bank of England and the Federal Reserve Bank of St Louis. He has published extensively in the areas of monetary economics and international economics. Among these publications are, for the IEA, *Too Much Money?*, with Gordon Pepper (Hobart Paper 68, 1975); *Independence for the Bank of England?*, with Forrest Capie and Terry Mills (Current Controversies 4, 1993); *The Right Road to Monetary Union Revisited*, with John Chown and Max Beber (Current Controversies 8, 1994); *Fifty Economics Fallacies Exposed* (Occasional Paper 129, 2002). He is a member of the IEA's Academic Advisory Council and a trustee of the Wincott Foundation.

FOREWORD

Financial regulation plays a vital role in the world economy. The bursting of the Internet and telecommunications bubble, a slowdown in world economic growth combined with war in Iraq and the uncertainties that preceded the war were some of the factors that led to falling equity prices over the three-year period to 2003. This fall in equity prices has put pressure on investment funds, insurance companies and pension schemes, highlighting the importance of prudential management of institutional investments. The collapse of major global companies such as Enron and Marconi has focused attention on weaknesses in corporate governance and led to calls for a strengthening of the mechanisms of regulatory oversight of our major companies. The pressures on the banking system in a number of countries, notably Japan, where the banking system has struggled with its bad loan portfolio for more than a decade, have underscored the importance of appropriate regulation of the banking system.

These recent developments are not without precedent: similar pressure, issues and concerns arose in the Great Depression. Such episodes are often followed by statutory regulatory reform: the 1930s saw the imposition of major regulatory limits on the US banking system, which greatly influenced the subsequent development of the US financial system up to the present day. But there is a danger that such regulatory reform addresses the previous problem, not the coming one. What is clear from history is that poor statutory regulation can cause considerable damage to the development of the financial system and the broader economy. What is less easy to establish, but is almost certainly the case, is that appropriate regulation can exert a quiet but important influence for good, helping the financial system to develop in a way that helps individuals and companies manage the risks and uncertainties that they face, thereby enhancing economic efficiency and well-being.

There is an important debate regarding the influence of the state in setting the regulatory framework. While there is no doubt that the events referred to above will lead to the evolution of regulation, should such regulation arise from governments and intergovernmental bodies or through the market itself? Regulation of the market itself can come through self-regulation, self-restraint or through the evolution of complex market regulatory mechanisms. The debate about the source of regulation is particularly important in discussing the failures of corporate governance because, arguably, those failures arose in countries in which corporate governance was subject to heavy, detailed statutory regulation.

Regulation is partly concerned with the prudential management of risk. It also concerns the potential conflicts of interest that can arise in a developed financial system, particularly when financial conglomerates have incentives to use information obtained in one part of the system to gain advantage in another part. It is also concerned with the scope of and limits on central banks and the authorities more generally to manage the economy so as to tame the worst swings in the economic cycle. This set of papers addresses a number of key aspects of these questions. (See the following Introduction for an overview.) The papers develop the ideas expressed in a series of lectures sponsored jointly by the Cass Business School and the Institute of Economic Affairs, presented at the Cass Business School in February 2003. These lectures brought together the leading thinkers and practitioners in the field of financial market regulation.

The Cass Business School serves as the business school of the City of London. Some 1,500 men and women from many different countries around the world graduate from it annually. Cass has the largest European grouping of academics specialising in finance and risk management, and many of its courses reflect this focus on finance, fitting with its mission to serve the needs of the City of London and financial markets more generally. Cass aims to serve as the intellectual hub of the City, promoting debates and forums where the issues facing the City and international financial markets more generally are addressed by City leaders and leading practitioners and academics.

The Institute of Economic Affairs, established in 1955, led much of the radical thinking associated with the rise of policies designed to transform the British economy over the last 25 years through the control of inflation, privatisation and liberalisation. It has been a major influence on the policy-making of successive UK governments and on governments around the world. It is therefore appropriate that the Cass Business School and the IEA should come together to promote discussion and education on the crucial issue of the regulation of financial markets.

By bringing together City leaders, practitioners and academics to focus on financial regulation, this annual lecture series will aim to help develop thinking on and analysis of the key issues facing regulators and the regulated alike. Financial regulation can exert a very major influence, whether for good or bad, and it therefore deserves major attention. If this series helps foster new and considered thinking as to how financial regulation should develop, then it will serve its purpose. Readings 58 expands on the subject matter of the lectures and will provide a timely but lasting aid to all those who need to understand better the subject of the regulation of financial markets.

As in all IEA publications, the views expressed in this book are those of the authors and not those of the Institute (which has no corporate view), its managing trustees, Academic Advisory Council members or senior staff.

PHILIP BOOTH

Editorial and Programme Director,
Institute of Economic Affairs
Professor of Insurance and Risk Management,
Cass Business School, City University

DAVID CURRIE

Dean
Cass Business School, City University

July 2003

FIGURES

The Regulation of Financial Markets

1 INTRODUCTION
Philip Booth

For many decades there has been a special body of law and regulations that relates to financial markets and financial transactions. For nearly 150 years, until the mid-1980s, that law broadly followed a consistent set of principles. Banks were treated as a special case within the financial architecture because of their crucial role in the payments system. For example, banks have long been required to follow authorisation procedures and maintain liquidity and capital ratios. Also, the special nature of long-term insurance was recognised in the deliberations of the 1853 Parliamentary Select Committee (see, for example, Nicholl, 1898). But even so, in the insurance field, unlike in the banking field, regulation was not, until recently, intrusive. Dealings in securities markets and in the capital markets, in which companies raise funds to finance their activities, have also long been regulated although, until recently, such regulation often arose from non-governmental sources, such as stock exchanges. Likewise, the closely related areas of accounting standards and corporate governance have traditionally been regulated through private institutions rather than through governmental authorities. Detailed statutory product regulation in financial services and the regulation of the product sales process is a relatively recent feature of the UK regulatory scene and mainly dates from the Financial Services Act 1986. Regulation of pension funds is also relatively recent and comes from a number of sources, including the authorities that give tax approval for pension schemes.

Thus regulation of financial markets now comes from a multiplicity of sources and is more detailed and more prescriptive (certainly in the UK) than has been the case in recent decades. There is also pressure for a growing standardisation of regulation on an international basis, as it is recognised that financial crises in one country can be transmitted through global markets to other countries. Another trend is that regulation has become so complex that research increasingly confines itself to narrow aspects of the subject and the broader view of the principles of regulation is frequently neglected. This can be dangerous. Practitioners, regulators and theoreticians as specialists in one narrow area may feel that a particular refinement to regulation may address a so-called 'market failure' in the area in which they are interested, without considering the damage that the proliferation of regulation can do to the operation of a market more generally.

Readings 58 *does* take a broader view. It does not cover every aspect of regulation (for example, there is very little discussion of product regulation). Particular aspects of financial regulation are covered elsewhere, including in other IEA work (see, for example, *Economic Affairs*, vol. 23, no. 3 for a discussion of product regulation; Sternberg (1998) for a discussion of corporate governance; and Myddelton (1995) for a discussion of accounting). However, Readings 58 does ask fundamental questions about the nature of regulation, the extent of regulation, the complexity of regulation, and the process of the development of international regulatory standards in banking, together with the management of financial crises.

The next four chapters of this monograph discuss financial

stability, financial crises and international regulation. Chapter 2 is a contribution from Howard Davies that both sets the scene and discusses the various different restraints on market participants which can help avoid financial crises. Davies emphasises the importance of market discipline, but he also believes that greater international coordination of regulation (particularly with regard to accounting standards) is necessary to avoid financial crises developing and being transmitted through the international financial system. Andrew Crockett argues that regulation needs to deal with the causes of financial instability, rather than just the symptoms. He suggests that there may be elements of market failure that need addressing through regulation and that the implementation of such regulation needs to have an international dimension. Geoffrey Wood takes a sceptical view of the need for wide-ranging international financial regulation. He believes that Crockett draws the definition of a financial crisis too widely. It is important, Wood argues, not to insulate institutions or individuals from the consequences of their own actions (a point that Howard Davies echoes). Nevertheless, there may be occasions when a central bank can be helpful in ensuring an orderly resolution to problems in financial markets, if such problems arise as a result of a lack of liquidity or inadequacies in the legal system: the problems in Long Term Capital Management in the late 1980s being such an example. However, Wood's prescription would not lead to a widening of the scope of regulatory action and would certainly not lead to intervention in volatile securities markets, as such intervention would tend to exacerbate rather than alleviate the problem of financial instability. Wood defines very precisely and relatively narrowly the appropriate scope of regulatory authority that is necessary within a banking system to prevent financial crises developing. Warwick

Lightfoot examines the relationship between price instability and financial instability. He stresses the importance of ensuring that there is ambiguity over the role of lender of last resort so that markets do not depend on the function. He is sceptical about whether an international lender of last resort could work.

The chapters by Lamfalussy, Booth, Ridley and Congdon look at the problem of financial regulation at a European Union (EU) level. Lamfalussy suggests that we should not react too hastily to recent corporate events such as the failure of Enron. Nor should such events change the prevailing view about the importance of integration of financial markets in the EU, which he believes should continue. However, Lamfalussy does suggest that the question of whether central banks should try to moderate booms and busts in financial markets should now be seriously considered, although he does not state his own view on this issue. This question is one that is also considered in the chapter by Wood in Readings 58 and also by Friedman and Goodhart (2003). Booth, Ridley and Congdon, in their chapters, question the approach to the integration of financial regulation in the EU. They suggest that forcing the pace of change through harmonisation of regulation is unnecessary in theory and damaging in practice. It is not necessary, they argue, to harmonise regulation in order to facilitate free trade, and there are many adverse affects of such harmonisation. Booth also discusses current regulatory developments in the insurance sector. Congdon makes the important point that discussion about the development of single European financial markets is perhaps ignoring the globalisation of financial markets that has taken place in the last 40 years. Congdon does, however, suggest that there are a limited number of areas where financial markets have not developed on a global basis and are unlikely to do so in the foreseeable future,

and where further integration at the EU level may bring benefits
– albeit relatively minor benefits.

References

Friedman, M., and Goodhart, C. A. E. (2003), *Money, Inflation
and the Constitutional Position of the Central Bank*, Readings 57,
Institute of Economic Affairs, London.

Myddelton, D. R. (1995), *Accountants without Standards?
Compulsion or evolution in company accounting*, Hobart Paper
128, Institute of Economic Affairs, London.

Nicholl, J. (1898), 'The Relation of the Actuarial Profession to the
State', *Journal of the Institute of Actuaries*, 34: 158.

Sternberg, E. (1998), *Corporate Governance: accountability in the
marketplace*, Hobart Paper 137, Institute of Economic Affairs,
London.

2 MANAGING FINANCIAL CRISES
Howard Davies

Introduction

Policyholders in Equitable Life, or investors in split capital investment trusts, may, with some reason, consider that their financial affairs have been thrown into crisis by the failings or failure of individual financial firms. Anyone with a sizeable stock market investment, whether direct or indirect, is aware that financial markets are going through an extremely difficult period. However, there has not been a financial crisis, in the proper sense of the word, in recent years. That is certainly the case if we define a crisis as a situation in which confidence in financial institutions or markets generally is lost, or where there is an actual, or a serious risk of, collapse in the whole financial system which would generate collateral damage even for savers and investors who are not directly linked to the institution or institutions that are the source of the crisis. Using that definition, it is some time since we experienced a full-blown financial crisis in the UK. Neither the collapse of BCCI nor that of Barings damaged confidence in the banking system as a whole. The secondary banking crisis of the early 1990s was perhaps a more direct threat to the stability of the system at the time. But there has been no need for the UK authorities to intervene on any substantial scale for some decades, and the losses to the various safety net protection schemes – the Deposit Protection Scheme, etc. – have been extremely modest.

That is not to say that we should be complacent, or that a financial crisis could not happen in the UK. Many people, when the term financial crisis is used, conjure up scenes of demonstrations by housewives banging saucepans in Argentina, hyperinflation in Brazil or Turkey, and wholesale bank failures in Russia. But the Scandinavian banking crisis of the late 1980s/early 1990s, Japan's decade-long, slow-burn financial sector meltdown, and especially the late 1990s failure of Long Term Capital Management (LTCM), which caused the Federal Reserve Bank of New York to promote a market-financed bail-out on the grounds of a possible systemic threat, remind us all that financial crises are not confined to emerging markets. The LTCM case (see also the chapter by Wood in this volume) also alerted us to the possibility that a systemic crisis might emerge from outside the banking system. Crises can arise in non-banks, and that is a powerful argument for an integrated approach to financial regulation.

The remainder of this chapter will reflect a little on recent crises and draw some conclusions as to how regulators should behave before, during and after a crisis. It will begin by offering a few thoughts on what can be done in the area of crisis prevention, and on managing crises once they have crystallised. Then the kinds of changes that have been implemented internationally in order to improve our ability to handle crises will be discussed in brief. Finally, additional steps that might be taken, and which could be both helpful and politically feasible, will be suggested.

Preventing financial crises

We cannot hope to eliminate international financial crises entirely: that might seem a depressing conclusion, but it is a realistic one. Liberalised global financial markets and the free flow of capital across borders bring with them the risks of over-shooting, greater volatility and imbalances that can exacerbate or amplify poor policy decisions. The result may be a currency crisis, a banking crisis or, worst of all, both. Reducing currency volatility by a return to fixed exchange rates, or even a gold standard, as advocated by some, and by tighter control of cross-border financial flows, might reduce the occurrence of international financial crises. Domestic crises could, however, still arise from poor fiscal and monetary policy decisions, and such crisis reduction would be at the cost of access to external finance and ultimately to economic growth. Also, financial liberalisation does mean that, if you throw a rock in the global financial pond, the ripples spread more quickly than otherwise: the viscosity of the water has reduced. But the pond is larger, the opportunities for risk sharing are greater, and enhanced transparency makes it harder for countries to persist in imprudent policies: the bubble is now pricked sooner. But whatever the regime, we will never entirely eliminate international financial crises.

There is an analogy here with the insistence at the Financial Services Authority (FSA) that we are not running a 'no-failure' regime. Failure is an inherent part of a flexible, competitive, innovative capitalist system. We should not aim to oversee a race in which all shall win prizes. Eliminating the possibility of failure would distort incentives and, in effect, penalise success. That is not to say, however, that a regulator should not attempt to reduce the number of failures, or deal properly with their consequences.

Quite the contrary – the FSA devotes considerable supervisory resources to attempting to reduce the number of firm failures and to mitigating the consequences of failure when it occurs. The FSA does this in the full knowledge that there will be companies which follow inappropriate business strategies, or that suffer from management incompetence or the lack of effective internal controls. Such firms will and should fail – despite our best efforts.

The same is true for financial crises. Whilst we cannot eliminate them, we can attempt to reduce their number, duration and spread and to mitigate the immediate consequences, particularly for innocent bystanders. In this task we have four principal tools at our disposal: international macroeconomic surveillance; market discipline; corporate governance; and prudential supervision. We might think of macroeconomic surveillance and market discipline operating at the macro level, while corporate governance and firm-specific prudential supervision operate at the micro level. But such distinctions are hardly waterproof and, properly used, each individual tool reinforces the others.

International macroeconomic surveillance

The Asian financial crisis of 1997–8 exposed some serious gaps in our global system of macroeconomic surveillance. How could a group of 'tiger economies' with good growth rates and relatively solid public finances suddenly fall like flies to financial speculators? We now know that a combination of fixed and rising foreign exchange rates, imprudent unhedged short-term dollar borrowing and long-term domestic currency lending (largely on real estate during a burgeoning asset bubble), combined with weak prudential oversight and corruption and cronyism, produced a lethal brew. How did the institutions tasked with international economic surveillance miss this explosive concoction?

I am sure this question will continue to be a subject of academic research for some time to come. So far, the preliminary analysis suggests that, for one thing, macrosurveillance overlooked the possibility that structural vulnerabilities such as poor regulatory structures could provoke or aggravate nascent financial crises. Institutions such as the International Monetary Fund (IMF), while always very strong on high-level macroeconomic analysis, lacked both market and regulatory expertise. Partly as a result, they failed to spot the pressures and imbalances that ultimately produced the Asian crisis. This failure provoked a considerable amount of soul-searching on the part of the IMF and the World Bank, in particular, which has generated some significant action.

Two institutional responses are worth highlighting. First, the G7 political leadership realised there were gaps in our global surveillance structure. Following a report drafted by Hans Tietmeyer, formerly head of Germany's Bundesbank, they established the Financial Stability Forum (FSF), which brings together high-level financial ministry officials, central bankers and regulators with a remit to both identify risk and vulnerabilities in the international financial system and set out mitigation strategies. The inclusion of regulators was a significant step, recognising the role of regulation in maintaining financial stability. The FSF is still, perhaps, finding its feet in the international financial architecture, but we in the UK have put a lot of effort into making it work, and the signs are positive.

Second, the IMF, recognising its own lacunae, has set out to improve its market and regulatory expertise. It has established a new Capital Markets Department under a former commercial banker

– Gerd Häusler of Dresdner – and has begun publishing a Global Financial Stability Review which has a significant influence on our own assessment of financial market risks. In addition, through its exhaustive Financial Sector Assessment Program (FSAP), the IMF is gaining knowledge of regulatory standards and structures that will be disseminated throughout the rest of the organisation.

The FSAP team carries out reviews of the financial sectors of individual member countries of the IMF, and indeed of some off-shore centres as well. The aim is to assess the extent to which each country is meeting international best practice standards of regulation and financial management. For example, a team of twenty or so experts visited the FSA three times in 2002 to carry out the UK review: it was a thorough process.

I should note that financial stability is also now on the European agenda, with heightened awareness of the linkages between financial firms and markets and developments in the real economy. Some have argued that the EU needs its own version of the FSF. The institutional structures are still being discussed. The outcome remains in doubt, partly because national arrangements for handling these issues remain very diverse. It is a challenge to create appropriate representative bodies at the EU level that accommodate regulatory diversity. Something concrete will emerge in due course, but exactly with which participants and with what scope, role and influence remains unclear: there is a gap that should be filled.

Market discipline

It would be wrong to think, however, that the regulators or the international institutions are the front line of defence against crisis.

In reality, markets are usually their own best regulators. This remains true despite their tendency to overreact and over-shoot. To perform this regulatory role, however, markets and market participants need timely and accurate information, and this leads to the complex issue of requirements for accounting standards, transparency and disclosure, as well as effective implementation and enforcement mechanisms.

Accounting remains the foundation upon which our entire financial system rests. If accounting and auditing standards are inappropriate, then transparency and good-quality disclosure are meaningless and supervision would be seriously challenged. We are gradually moving towards internationally accepted norms, through the work of the International Accounting Standards Board. The European Commission has already agreed that International Accounting Standards should be adopted by all listed European corporations by 2005. Assuming that we achieve transatlantic convergence with American generally accepted accounting principles (GAAP), ultimately we will have an agreed basis upon which to assess companies, regardless of the location of their headquarters, or of where their stock is traded. There are some fundamental disagreements, often between national agencies, on key issues such as the use of fair value accounting and expensing stock options, but I am cautiously optimistic that this work will eventually produce an acceptable result.

More generally, there has been considerable work internationally on developing, refining and implementing the various codes and standards that markets will use to assess firms and countries. The FSF has approved a core list of twelve key Codes and Standards which stretch across banking, securities, insurance, fiscal transparency, payments systems, money laundering and offshore centres, etc. The sectoral standard-setters have increasingly realised that the key issue is not the standard-making but rather effective implementation. So in organisations such as the International Organisation of Securities Commissions (IOSCO) and the International Association of Insurance Supervisors (IAIS), effort is focusing on methodologies to help members implement good practices in their countries.

In the end, however, little will be gained if market participants themselves do not actively use the internationally agreed standards in their day-to-day judgements. Here we face the difficulty of transforming a qualitative standard into a useful quantitative reference point. The IMF has recognised this challenge and, assisted by the Bank of England and the FSA, has embarked on a programme to ensure that codes and standards are increasingly 'user friendly'.

Corporate governance

There is much overlap between the development of codes and standards for markets and the standards that firms should use in their internal control systems. The recent scandals in the USA, in particular, have exposed some serious gaps in areas such as auditor oversight and independence, the role of boards in overseeing management, corporate disclosure, conflicts of interest, etc. The controversial Sarbanes-Oxley Act in the USA is meant to address some of these shortcomings. On this side of the Atlantic, we continue to stress the responsibilities of senior management for the correct and timely disclosure of pertinent information and the necessity of establishing robust internal control systems to ensure that problems are caught before they become unmanageable, with possible catastrophic effects for the firm, its employees, investors and perhaps the larger financial system.

Internationally, the Organisation for Economic Cooperation and Development (OECD) is currently working on a revision of its Guidelines for Corporate Governance which, although only guidelines, spell out basic acceptable norms. Corporate governance issues do have a particular political resonance, especially in the light of some of the salary excesses and performance failures exposed by recent scandals.

Prudential supervision

But in spite of the emphasis that is placed on the role of market discipline, robust prudential supervision of both firms and markets is essential. Such supervision must be risk-based. That is to say resources, which are always finite, must be allocated to those areas where there is the greatest risk and the greatest impact. This approach has implications for both investors and consumers, the most basic of which is that investors and consumers must take greater responsibility for their financial decisions. The risk-based approach of the FSA means that attention is, or should be, focused on those key institutions or interfaces that have the most impact. But not everything can be covered by a regulator. Sophisticated financial markets also require smart and educated consumers and investors, and consumer education is an area where we are investing considerably more resources than most of our regulatory counterparts, though both the US and Australian regulators have already done a lot to raise consumer understanding of financial issues.

The FSA is an integrated regulator covering banking, insurance and securities. In a world of accelerating cross-sector and cross-border financial innovation, universal banks, bulge-bracket investment banks and insurance-company-owned banks, the FSA believes in an integrated approach. It allows the FSA, almost naturally, to practise consolidated supervision, i.e. to practise a comprehensive approach to the firms it regulates and all their sub-entities.

In theory, and increasingly in practice, as the FSA develops its integrated approach, it is able to gain a better understanding of the interaction between different types of risk in different sectors of the market. The FSA can better understand the overall risk dynamics of complex diversified institutions. One of the key tasks which all FSA line supervisors are required to undertake in relation to the larger firms within our care is to assess the potential impact of the failure of that institution on other firms, on its customers and on the markets more generally. This impact assessment could not be carried out effectively by the previous sector-based regulators.

In all these ways, regulators have made some progress in understanding the sources of financial instability and in setting up mechanisms to allow that information to be more effectively shared across borders. But problems will slip through the net, inevitably. So it is appropriate also to ask whether corresponding progress has been made in our ability to manage crises when they arise.

Managing financial crises

Regulators are probably still better at identifying financial crises, especially when they are about to burst upon them, than managing them. But progress is being made. If the recent Argentinian debt default had occurred five years ago it is likely that the contagion effects on Argentina's neighbours and global financial markets would have been much greater. To a degree the lack of contagion reflects better risk management by the major international banks. They saw an unsustainable position and lowered their exposure. But it also, to some degree, reflects improvements in the 'plumbing' of the international financial system. Greater sophistication and differentiation between markets has led to implicit 'tiering' by investors which will reduce contagion at the cost of making it harder for those with a poor policy mix to borrow money on global capital markets.

Nevertheless, the management of financial crises can be a chaotic and painful business which perhaps could be done better. The Mexican, Asian, Russian and Brazilian experiences of the late 1990s have provoked a series of reform proposals which range from plans for a supranational World Financial Authority to making the IMF the global lender of last resort (see the chapter by Lightfoot in this volume) or transforming it into the overseer of an international bankruptcy court modelled on US-style Chapter 11 proceedings. The arguments behind some of these suggestions are at times persuasive but, to date at least, they all lack political feasibility. For the moment, or at least until the next major international crisis, national governments will remain unwilling to cede even greater powers to international institutions. We are therefore likely to have the post-Asian crisis institutional structure and division of responsibilities for some time to come. The debate over some form of international bankruptcy process is not yet concluded and may yet produce something new, but the grander schemes are unlikely to get the political support necessary to take them forward. This should not, however, be interpreted as saying that nothing further can be done to improve our ability to manage financial crises after they have broken out.

Steps taken to date to improve crisis management

It is fashionable to argue that the international response to the Asian financial crisis has been inadequate, and indeed that the reaction to the gaps highlighted by the Enron and WorldCom scandals has been slow and insufficient. I do not take such a pessimistic view. At the institutional level the FSF is now actively engaged in vulnerability, risk, gap and 'underlap' identification, and increasingly in developing strategies for risk mitigation. The IMF and Bank for International Settlements (BIS) have attempted to counter the perception that they are 'Eurocentric' by establishing offices in Tokyo (the IMF) and Hong Kong and Mexico (the BIS) respectively. The IMF, through the creation of the Capital Markets Department, has consciously set out to improve its market and regulatory capabilities. Better coordination between international financial institutions, another flaw underscored by the Asian crisis, is now on everyone's agenda.

In terms of policy, crawling currency pegs are largely discredited. One of the understandings to emerge out of the Asian crisis is the need for a well-thought-out sequencing of reforms intended to liberalise financial flows, and that those reforms in turn must be combined with solid regulatory structures. More recently, the latest bout of chaos in Argentina has demonstrated that even currency boards cannot hold back speculators if policy choices are fundamentally flawed.

At a less exalted level, but probably more importantly, we are cleaning up, or flushing out, a lot of our international financial plumbing. A few examples illustrate this process. At the international committee level, following the collapse of Enron, IOSCO quickly proposed new principles on auditor independence and oversight and corporate transparency which are likely to become the global standards. The FSA have just published a consultation paper on financial market conflicts of interest and the UK Listing Authority, now a division of the FSA, will be looking at various corporate governance issues as part of its current review of the UK listing rules.

As an integrated regulator, the FSA is particularly cognisant of the increasing complexity innovation has brought to the financial sector. Recent advances in debt securitisation and risk transfer, particularly between the banking and insurance sectors, have raised the linked questions of where certain risks are lodged and whether they have been correctly priced. As issues like credit risk transfer become more important to the FSA, it works both directly with the financial industry and through appropriate international committees such as the FSF and the IAIS to obtain a better understanding of the extent of any possible problems. So far, there are signs that credit risk transfer has, overall, been a stabilising factor, but there are concerns about whether some of the buyers of credit risk have properly assessed the risks they have taken on.

Similarly, recent financial developments have resulted in the creation of very large, very complex financial firms, known as large complex financial institutions (LCFIs), which are not necessarily all American. If one of these firms got into serious trouble and had to be unwound there would be grave problems. To prepare for any eventuality the FSA and other regulators have expended considerable effort on improving their understanding of LCFIs, their structures and risk management and control systems. This is still very much 'work in progress', but at a minimum regulators now have a better understanding of the challenges they would face if things were to go wrong and an orderly run-down became necessary. There would be no simple, neat answers in such an eventuality.

The European Financial Groups Directive will bring a measure of consolidated supervision to all financial conglomerates operating in Europe when it is implemented in 2005, and there is also the commitment to implementing International Accounting Standards during the same year. The conclusion of the Basel Committee negotiations on capital adequacy, which will be transmuted into European law through a new capital adequacy directive, will introduce a greater risk-based element to the calculation of bank capital. Through its FSAPs and its offshore centre assessments, the IMF is both assessing jurisdictions against minimum standards and gaining for itself a much more refined view of where structural pressures could manifest themselves. IOSCO and the Committee on Clearing and Payments Systems (CPSS, a sub-group of the Basel Banking Supervisory Committee) have just published a useful joint study on where problems could arise in the international payments system.

It is reasonable to ask, 'Is this enough?' and, 'Has the international community responded adequately to the challenges, or is there more to do?' We will not be able to give wholly convincing answers to these questions until the next crisis presents itself, at which point it will be too late.

Looking ahead: what more can be done?

We cannot yet judge the effectiveness of the most recent reforms following on from the Enron and Argentinian crises. Some useful steps have been taken in response to the exposure of corporate excesses or tensions within the international financial system. More time, however, is needed to determine whether they will be fully effective. For its part, France has made it clear that socially responsible markets, corporate governance and excessive market volatility will be a central part of the agenda for their presidency of the 2003 G7/G8 economic summit process. This year, regulatory issues will be highlighted as never before by both heads of government and finance ministers at the Evian summit.

But what useful outcomes could there be, if one accepts that there is no political consensus for any significant new international institutions or even for any significant increase in the powers of existing institutions? Even within those constraints more can be done to reduce the occurrence of financial crises, lessen their impact and speed up their resolution. Foremost, we have to push forward convergence on a single set of international accounting standards. There are some difficult problems to be addressed, including issues such as the treatment of financial instruments, the expensing of stock options and the disclosure of pension fund deficits. These are difficult questions that have bedevilled national standard-setters for years and will be even more difficult to agree on internationally. And yet recent events, which suggest that US standard-setters have no monopoly on wisdom, have created an environment where real progress can be made towards a single set of standards which would allow cross-border comparisons. There is a new willingness in the USA to consider compromises, and we should seize this opportunity.

There are other actions that would help the management of financial crises. One example is the inclusion of Collective Action

Clauses (CACs) in all sovereign bond contracts, which would prevent a rump of disaffected investors from holding up debt restructuring. This is already the case in London for 30 per cent of the sovereign bond market, and it seems a pity that extension globally is delayed because of post-Great Depression attitudes enshrined in US domestic bankruptcy legislation. More work also needs to be done on options for international debt restructuring, including standstill arrangements that would contribute to orderly dispute resolution. In addition, recent work on financial stability indicators has begun to bear fruit. Such devices could provide both national governments and international agencies with a useful early warning before pressures build up to explosion point.

On the policy front, we need to go farther on both crisis prevention and crisis management. Those organisations such as the FSF and IMF that have surveillance responsibilities should be willing to speak out both on vulnerability issues and on mitigation strategies, regardless of the sensibilities of powerful members: only then will they meet their full potential. In this vein, greater clarity in the mandates of international organisations identifying vulnerabilities, setting standards and assessing and, if necessary, enforcing standard implementation needs to be fostered. Institutions and their national members have to be willing to transform their judgements into concrete actions. Work towards this end is progressing in IOSCO, IAIS and elsewhere, but it has to be still further encouraged.

Work on upgrading and implementing internationally agreed codes and standards will continue. What is required, however, is a far greater emphasis on effective implementation. As noted above, for this to happen standards must be made more 'user friendly'. Also, the IMF is gathering a mass of information and experience on how these standards are being implemented through its FSAP and Offshore Centre Assessment Programs. To date, these programs remain entirely voluntary and, for the moment, are not supposed to influence either the IMF's or the private sector's lending decisions. Changing this is a sensitive and controversial matter, especially for emerging markets, but somehow a means must be found to draw on information related to adherence to internationally agreed codes and standards to influence both public and private lending practices. It is not unreasonable to expect that jurisdictions participating in and benefiting from global financial flows meet and continue to adhere to minimum financial sector standards and, ideally, best practice. As a first step, the FSAP country assessments should routinely be published. The UK will shortly set an example and make the full IMF assessment public. Publication will help market participants draw their own conclusions about financial stability, and the integrity of the financial sector, which could itself enhance market discipline.

Conclusion

A stable international financial system is merely a means to an end. That end is sustainable economic growth and rising prosperity. Stable domestic and international financial markets are therefore necessary but not sufficient conditions for continued sustainable growth. Recent financial crises have starkly shown the damage that poor regulatory structures and oversight can do to countries with ostensible positive growth rates. We have come a long way since Mexico in 1995, the first of the 'new round' of financial crises. We still have a way to go, however, before we have in place the systems, institutions, policies and levers that will mini-mise the number, duration, fall-out and complexity of financial crises. Elimination of financial crises is beyond our reach; but we can realistically aim to do a better job of preventing and managing them in the future.

3 STRENGTHENING FINANCIAL STABILITY
Andrew Crockett

Introduction

The subject of this paper is financial stability: what it means; why it is important; why it has, arguably, become more difficult to achieve; and what can be done about it.

Financial stability can be defined as the situation in which the capacity of financial institutions and markets to efficiently mobilise savings, provide liquidity and allocate investment is maintained unimpaired. Financial stability is distinguishable from monetary stability, although the two are often complementary. Monetary stability is usually taken to mean stability in the overall value of money – or low and stable inflation. Financial stability means the absence of strains that curtail the intermediation function of the financial system, such as the failure of the banking payments system. Financial stability can be consistent with the periodic failure of individual financial institutions, and with fluctuations of prices in markets for financial assets. The failure of individual institutions is of concern only if it leads, as it sometimes can, to an impairment of the basic intermediation role of the financial system at large. And asset price volatility is of concern only if it leads to a severe misallocation of capital.

Why is financial stability important?

Twenty-five years ago, the dominant monetary and financial issue facing the industrial world was the control of inflation. In 1980, consumer price increases in the OECD countries, though lower than their peak, still averaged over 10 per cent per annum and seemed to be heading higher. Inflation was having serious social and political, as well as economic, consequences. It had proved remarkably resistant to policies adopted to combat it. By contrast, the issue of financial instability scarcely registered as a major concern of policy-makers. There had been isolated episodes of strain, such as the secondary banking crisis in the UK, and failures of individual institutions, such as Bankhaus Herstatt in Germany and Franklin National Bank in New York. None of these, however, had created wider financial or economic consequences, which are the mark of a serious financial stability problem.

A quarter of a century later, there has been a remarkable evolution. Thanks to resolute action by central banks, the battle against inflation has been largely successful. Meanwhile the problem of financial instability has moved up the policy agenda. On the face of it, this is strange. Why has price stability not yielded a 'peace dividend' of greater financial stability? And why has financial turmoil proved so troublesome to manage? This paper will make the following interrelated points about the causes of and appropriate reactions to greater financial instability.

First, following a wave of financial liberalisation, the financial system has come to play a much larger role in the allocation of resources than was the case 25 years ago. The capacity of financial system weaknesses to generate strains and even crises has therefore grown, as have the real economic consequences when the system malfunctions. Second, there are elements in the functioning of financial markets that naturally tend to overreaction. This 'fear and greed' phenomenon is not driven simply by human nature, although this should not be underestimated, but also by elements specific to the dynamics of financial markets. Third, while a stable monetary environment helps the efficient functioning of the financial system in many respects, it may not be sufficient to eliminate these tendencies to excess. In one respect, indeed, it may even encourage them. Confidence in the power of the authorities to manage the economy can encourage excessive risk taking, if economic agents come to take insufficient account of downside risks. Fourth, greater stability can be achieved through a supervisory approach that harnesses the prudential aspects of market disciplines. This means that the behavioural norms and prudential standards incorporated in systemic oversight need to focus on providing accurate financial *information* to market participants, and a framework of *incentives* that encourages a proper weighting of downside risks. Finally, there is a need to strengthen the macro-prudential (or system-wide) aspects of the supervisory framework, including the way in which standards and codes are implemented. We must be aware of the risk that even individually rational and prudent behaviour can at times become systemically destabilising.

The growing role of financial intermediation

As has just been noted, one reason for the increased importance of financial stability is the fact that the financial system now plays a greater role in resource allocation than it did 25 years ago. There have been many contributory factors to this development, but it is helpful to think of the main driving forces as being those of liberalisation and technological innovation. Liberalisation, in turn, has been driven both by the ascent of the free market philosophy and by the sheer impracticability of maintaining restrictions and controls in the face of technological innovation.

Liberalisation has affected many aspects of economic life, but the main developments of relevance to the financial sector can be listed as follows:

(i) The reduction in the role of the state in economic activity through privatisation and the lifting of administrative controls;
(ii) the removal of impediments, direct and indirect, to competition between financial institutions;
(iii) the removal of restrictions on the pricing of financial transactions, such as rates of interest paid and received by banks; and
(iv) the removal of restrictions on international capital movements and the widespread introduction of currency convertibility.

Technology has affected the financial sector in two ways: first, by reducing the cost of processing and communicating information; and second, through the development of new instruments for the measurement and management of financial risk. A dramatic reduction in the cost of financial intermediation has not only drawn new users into the system (that is, ultimate savers and borrowers) but, even more dramatically, encouraged a greater *intensity* of financial intermediation (that is, more intermediate transactions between the ultimate saver and borrower). The development of new financial instruments has enabled a quantum leap in the scope of risk management – an advance that has facilitated risk taking as well as risk shedding.

The impact of technology and liberalisation on the role of the financial system has been compounded by two other trends in Western societies. One is growing levels of personal wealth, and the other is the ageing of populations. Together, these trends have resulted in greater volumes of financial savings seeking outlets in the capital markets and in financial intermediaries.

The growing role of the financial sector in the allocation of resources has significant potential advantages for the efficiency with which our economies function. If financial markets work well, they will direct resources to their most productive uses, as measured by relative rates of return adjusted for risk. Risks will be more accurately priced and will be borne by those most willing and able to bear them. Real economic activity will proceed with fewer financial uncertainties. Investment should increase in quantity and improve in quality as a result.

There is another side to the coin, however. The fact that our economies have become more dependent on their financial systems means that, if the financial system malfunctions, the adverse consequences are likely to be more severe than they used to be. The past decade or so has provided ample evidence of the costs of financial instability. At the international level, there has been the Mexican crisis of 1994–95; the East Asian crisis of 1997–98; and the Argentinian crisis that began in 2001 and is still far from reaching its end.

At the national level, there are also examples of costly financial instability in advanced countries. These include: banking crises in Spain and the Nordic countries in the 1980s; the savings and loan crisis in the USA; and the financial bubble in Japan, the costs of which are still being felt today. Closer to home, if one defines financial instability broadly, there was the ERM crisis of 1992. Also, the recovery of the USA from the recession of the early 1990s was delayed by financial 'headwinds' resulting from strained balance sheets.

The stability/instability properties of financial markets

The growing role of financial markets does not by itself explain why financial instability has become more prevalent. So it is worth considering in more detail why open financial markets have proved vulnerable to periodic episodes of stress. As Western countries embarked on the process of liberalising their financial markets, little thought was given to the possibility that this might result in an increase in financial instability. It was generally assumed that in financial markets, as in those for other goods and services, open competition would produce stable equilibrium prices. If, in addition, low inflation could be achieved, that would further support overall financial stability.

This view did not take into account some particular characteristics of financial markets that differentiate them from the conventional model of equilibrium price determination. In financial markets, fundamental value is extremely hard to assess. We can define a financial asset's value as the product of its expected flow of income, a discount rate and a risk premium. But this does not get us very far. The key element in judging the value of a financial asset is how much it can be sold for in the market. A function of financial claims is to telescope into the present intrinsically uncertain cash flow streams. In assessing these uncertainties, there are strong psychological incentives to extrapolate recent experience, and to fall victim to current fashions about how assets should be valued.

Such partial vision is true of individual agents taken in isolation. It is even stronger in the social behavioural patterns reflected in market prices. Price reactions to 'news' can go through phases in which, whatever the intrinsic information content, the news is interpreted as reinforcing the prevailing paradigm. The 'new economy' euphoria of the late 1990s is only the most recent example of such a phenomenon.

The process by which equilibrium is maintained in the financial sector does not work in quite the same way as in other industries. Normally, we think of supply and demand curves as being well behaved. The increased supply of a product exerts downward pressure on its price, thus limiting the eventual increase in supply. In the case of credit, however, an expansion in supply can, for a time, strengthen economic activity and boost asset prices. By improving the balance sheet position of both borrowers and lenders, it can sustain further increases in the supply of credit. Excess capacity and risk can build up partly unnoticed. The mutually re-inforcing process between perceived wealth and access to external funding masks the extent of the underlying financial imbalance, until the process, when it goes too far, at some point unwinds. The amplitude of the financial cycle is thereby augmented.

These problems are exacerbated by the fact that the leverage inherent in financial intermediation can give rise to fragile balance sheet structures. The sudden and sometimes indiscriminate retrenchment of suppliers of funds can cause institutions and markets to be starved of liquidity, intensifying price declines and impairing the functioning of markets. Bank runs are the textbook example. But there are also cases of securities markets functioning in a similar way. In the wake of the Long Term Capital Management crisis, for example, liquidity virtually dried up for a while, and the financial system was perilously close to a full-blown crisis.

Financial stability problems can also arise from the moral hazard problems caused by the official protection put in place in response to past episodes of financial instability. These can weaken market discipline without providing offsetting prudential incentives.

While the above characteristics are inherent in financial activity, and in the institutional safeguards put in place in the first half of the twentieth century, a number of changes in the financial regime over the past 25 years have arguably increased the potential for financial instability. All of them can ultimately be traced back to the financial liberalisation and technological innovation that have gathered pace during the period. This process has resulted in a broader range of services, at lower prices and more accessible terms than ever before. But these significant benefits have not come for free. It is worth considering four implications of financial liberalisation and technological innovation for financial stability.

First, competitive pressures have vastly increased. This means that the rents that licensed financial institutions could previously extract from their protected franchises have diminished, if not disappeared altogether. The cushion available to absorb mistakes or misfortune has become much thinner. Previously sheltered financial institutions have had to learn to manage risk more actively, with a smaller margin for mistakes. Frequently, they have had to compete with new entrants, not saddled with burdensome cost structures inherited from the past. Net operating margins have thus come under pressure, making it harder to earn a given return for the same amount of risk. Consequently, the incentives to enhance returns by taking on added risk have grown.

Second, the new environment has structurally increased liquidity and the potential for leverage. The development of new financial instruments, and financial engineering more generally, has made it easier for both financial and non-financial firms to realise value from assets, whether tangible or intangible. This has, in a sense, made liquid a wider range of income streams and by the same token increased the potential for leverage. Moreover, the hugely increased emphasis on stock market value has encouraged the exploitation of leverage. In a rising market, leverage is the winning formula. If the period of rising asset prices is protracted, market participants can come to forget the warning that regulators now insist be included in the small print of stock offerings: 'Prices can go down as well as up'.

Third, the new environment has tended to raise the option value implicit in safety nets. The reason is simple. *Ceteris paribus*, guarantees become more valuable as the environment becomes riskier. So the hidden subsidy provided by the official sector has become greater, and the danger of resource misallocation through the mispricing of risk has grown.

Finally, financial globalisation has transformed geography, with significant implications for the character of instability. Globalisation has heightened the significance of common factors in originating and spreading financial distress. It has done so by extending and tightening financial linkages across institutions, markets and countries; by increasing the uniformity of the information set available to economic agents; and by encouraging greater similarity in the assessment of that information. Freedom of capital movements has exposed emerging market countries to potential volatility of access to external funding. Portfolio adjustments that are comparatively minor for institutions in the countries originating capital flows can be of first-order significance for the recipients. This greatly increases the recipients' vulnerability to changes in sentiment, whether these are due to revised perceptions of economic conditions in the periphery or to developments at the core.

Some of the environmental changes I have just described are particularly acute during the transition from a sheltered to a liberalised environment. Others may have a more permanent character. The overall conclusion is that market discipline alone may be insufficient to ensure the desirable degree of financial stability. Hence the issue of whether additional policy action is needed to protect the system against instability needs to be raised. But before this question is discussed it is worth commenting on the link between financial instability and the monetary regime.

Why has price stability not produced financial stability?

It is not uncommon for economists and financial practitioners to argue that monetary stability should yield, as a by-product, improved financial stability. There is much validity in this contention. Inflation has always provided fertile ground for resource misallocation and facilitated the build-up of over-extended balance sheets. Inflation makes it harder to distinguish between real and nominal magnitudes. Moreover, since *high* inflation is almost invariably associated with *unstable* inflation, the expectations on which financial judgements are based are rendered even more difficult to form with confidence.

However, it would not be right to say that price stability is a sufficient criterion for financial stability. There are numerous counter-examples, of which the Japanese and East Asian cases are only the most prominent.

Two possible factors help explain why financial instability seems to persist, even in a world in which price stability has been credibly established. One lies in the paradox that success in taming inflation can make economies even more vulnerable to those waves of excessive optimism that breed unsustainable asset price dynamics. A danger sign is the increased prevalence in upswings of articles heralding the 'end of the business cycle'. In such circumstances, many may come to believe that low inflation removes a frequent cause of the termination of economic expansions, namely a sharp tightening of monetary policy. They may thus be tempted to accept balance sheet structures that are particularly vulnerable to changes in financial conditions.

The second possible factor is a more controversial conjecture. It is the following: in a monetary regime in which the central bank's operational objective is expressed *exclusively* in terms of short-term inflation, there may be insufficient protection against that build-up of financial imbalances that lies at the root of much of the financial instability we observe. This could be so if the focus on short-term inflation control meant that the authorities did not tighten monetary policy sufficiently pre-emptively to guard against excessive credit expansion and asset price increases. In the jargon, if the monetary policy reaction function does not incorporate financial imbalances, the monetary anchor may fail to deliver financial stability.

One response to this conundrum could be to modify, at least at the margin, the monetary strategy. This is a highly controversial matter, and space does not permit a full discussion here. However, if the monetary anchor is, along with conventional market forces, insufficient to produce financial stability, then additional policies may be needed to achieve these objectives. Such policies may include the design of prudential standards and codes to enhance the stability of the financial system.

Standards and codes for greater financial stability

In principle, a competitive financial system should eventually eliminate poorly performing institutions or market platforms, and should encourage the development of prudent and efficient practices. In other words, competition should foster convergence towards best practice in risk management. For various reasons, however, this may not happen, or may not happen quickly enough. Hence the justification for official oversight of the financial sector, to strengthen prudential management.

Prudential supervision of financial institutions has a long history. In the past, financial sector regulation tended to focus on the authorisation of financial institutions, on the definition of their permitted spheres of activity, and on required balance sheet ratios. More recently, however, growing attention has been devoted to the prudential management of risk.

There is growing recognition that the most effective regulatory framework is one that works with the grain of market forces, and allows the greatest play to market disciplines. Hence the search to relate regulatory requirements to risk management practices, and to find ways to increase transparency.

It is also increasingly accepted that globalisation of financial activity means that prudential norms have to be internationally consistent. Otherwise, the twin risks of regulatory arbitrage and competition in laxity are likely to present themselves. The international dimension of standards and codes raises the issue of how such standards should be developed, a subject that will be discussed below.

It is now recognised that efficient financial intermediation requires a high-quality financial infrastructure, that is, the network of the conventions, practices and information that underlie market activity. This includes the systems of contract law and law enforcement, bankruptcy procedures, the accounting framework and auditing standards, corporate governance practices, and requirements for transparency and data dissemination.

It has also been realised that prudential standards are interdependent. Minimum capital requirements for banks are of little use if the accounting conventions used to value a bank's assets and liabilities are flawed. And accounting conventions are only as good as the auditing standards used to apply them. More generally, market discipline requires accurate information, a legal environment that provides adequate security to market participants, and a payments system that can be relied on.

These underlying trends in the prudential oversight of the financial system have come together in the international effort to develop a framework of codes and standards for the financial sector. This effort crystallised in the wake of the Asian crisis, and owes much to the forceful advocacy of the UK Chancellor of the Exchequer in his capacity as chairman of the IMF's International Monetary and Financial Committee.

The strategy in the development of that international framework is: first, to define those areas of financial activity in which it is desirable to develop internationally agreed standards of best practice; second, to assign the role of standard-setting to an appropriate international grouping; and third, to devise mechanisms that foster convergence on this best practice by the widest possible range of countries.

The scope of standards

It has just been argued that the financial sector is marked by a considerable degree of interdependence and complementarity. This suggests a broad scope for standards. Standards can be grouped in three main areas. First, guidelines for supervision of the main types of financial intermediary – banks, securities issuers and insurance companies. Second, standards for the transparent disclosure of the financial information needed to facilitate the efficient performance of markets – macroeconomic information provided by governments, and microeconomic information related to the financial position of market participants and their counter-parties. Third, codes for the robust underpinning of market infrastructure – standards for contract law and law enforcement, corporate governance, accounting conventions, auditing practices, safety and soundness in the payment system, and so on.

Who should set the standards?

Since standards are comprehensive in scope, interdependent in nature and global in their impact, it might seem logical to have a single authority responsible for their formulation. Some, including John Eatwell, have put the case on these grounds for a 'World Financial Authority' with broad powers of regulatory design and supervisory oversight. There is some logic in this idea, but as a matter of sheer politics it does not seem that it will be practically feasible for quite some time to come. A more promising approach is to assign the responsibility for developing standards in individual areas to groups of national experts. In this way, the relevance of the resulting standards is enhanced and their acceptability in national jurisdictions is strengthened. However, means must be sought to ensure that the resulting standards represent a convergence to best practice and not a lowest common denominator.

How should standards be implemented?

The experience of the Basel Committee on Banking Supervision is instructive in helping us understand the mechanisms by which standards should be implemented. The Basel Committee is composed of senior supervisors from the most advanced countries, and has issued supervisory guidance on a wide range of topics. Basel Committee recommendations have no legal force. But since they have been adopted by consensus, they have been applied in all countries represented on the committee. Interestingly, they have also been almost universally applied in non-member countries – a telling example of the power of peer pressure and market forces to promote the adoption of best practice and to enforce what has been called 'soft law'.

The success of the Basel Committee process is not just an academic matter of securing a common regulatory approach. It has produced real economic benefits. It is arguable that the absence of significant difficulties in the banking systems of Europe and America in the past couple of years, despite significant economic shocks, owes much to the strengthening of risk management that has taken place under the aegis of the Basel Committee's standards.

Realistically, of course, peer pressure will not be sufficient, by itself, to secure the prompt implementation of the wide range of standards that have now been drawn up. The international institutions, principally the IMF and the World Bank, have an important role to play here. They are using their consultation missions with member countries to carry out Financial Sector Assessment Programs (FSAPs) and Reports on Standards and Codes (ROSCs). FSAPs and ROSCs are a key means of enabling countries to 'benchmark' their current standards on international best practice, to identify weaknesses, and to devise means for dealing with them. Giving publicity to the state of a country's financial sector may, of course, be the best way to ensure that the market is able to reward progress, through greater access to finance, on more favourable terms.

Micro-prudential and macro-prudential oversight

Improved risk management at the level of individual institutions can go a long way to strengthening the resilience of the system at large. But, by itself, it may not be quite enough. As has been noted above, the dynamics of financial markets can introduce inherent pro-cyclicality into market behaviour. How can this be dealt with?

The first step is clearly to understand the underlying causes of this pro-cyclicality. In part, it lies in the short-term nature of many risk measures. Risk measurement is often based on assessments of the recent past and the immediate future. Risk comparisons are made at a point in time on the basis of how an institution compares with its peers. But risk has a time-dimensional as well as a cross-sectional character. Existing techniques of risk assessment arguably pay insufficient attention to the movement of risk through the cycle, and the evolution of common risk exposures.

With the benefit of hindsight, we can see that risks tend to *accumulate* during the upswing of a cycle, then to *materialise* when the economy turns down. At the time, however, risks may appear to be diminishing the longer the economic expansion continues. In other words, conventional risk management tools lack the capacity to identify the emerging over-extension of balance sheets at a system-wide level.

Another limitation of an institutional focus in risk management lies in the interdependence of the actions and assessments of market participants. Risk models typically treat the external environment as independent of the actions of the entity managing risk. In fact, however, not only are some players large enough to have an impact on markets by themselves, many use similar models to guide their behaviour. This means that 'one-way markets' can develop more easily than theory would suggest. Thus, what is sensible and rational for an individual market participant acting in isolation may produce a destabilising outcome for the market as a whole.

A couple of simple examples can help to make the point. When a lending institution faces a possible slowdown in economic activity, it may seek to cut back its lending activities to reduce its risk exposure. Of course, if all lenders act in the same way, they may well produce the result they are seeking to protect themselves against. A similar process can take place in markets for traded assets. If an external shock produces a downward price adjustment, the consequent increase in measured Value at Risk (VaR) may produce further sales, additional downward movements in asset prices, further increases in VaR, and so on.

It is not easy to find solutions for these problems. Nevertheless, some avenues offer useful prospects. It would be good for financial institutions to adopt risk management practices that take better account of the evolution of risk over time. Techniques such as through-the-cycle credit assessment and pre-provisioning may have a role to play here. Second, supervisors should encourage the use of stress testing to assess the vulnerability of institutions to extreme events. They may also need to think about how the information from stress tests at individual institutions can be aggregated for the system as a whole. In other words, how might endogenous reactions to exogenous shocks amplify disturbances in potentially troublesome ways? Third, it may be desirable to develop oversight structures that enable the authorities to track emerging vulnerabilities in the financial system. Many central banks, like the Bank of England, now issue 'Financial Stability Reviews' and the Treasury, the Bank of England and the FSA have regular meetings to consider potential areas of weakness in the financial system.

Something similar has taken place at the international level. Following the Asian crisis, and as part of their search for a 'new financial architecture', the ministers and governors of the G7 countries established the Financial Stability Forum (FSF). This brings together, at a very senior level, the key authorities responsible for international financial stability. They comprise: the finance ministries, central banks and regulatory authorities from the countries with the largest financial markets; the main international organisations (IMF, World Bank, BIS and OECD); and the principal standard-setting bodies (the Basel Committee, the International Accounting Standards Board, IOSCO and others).

The FSF has not, perhaps, captured the public imagination through dramatic crisis intervention. Nevertheless, it has done much useful work in focusing attention on common sources of financial vulnerability, and in providing an impetus for tackling them. Perhaps even more importantly, the FSF is welding together institutions and groupings that need to work increasingly closely to promote financial market efficiency and stability. This is a promising tool of international cooperation that can, and should, be further developed in the years ahead.

Conclusion

We have come a long way in the past 25 years in understanding the way in which a liberalised financial system works and its vulnerability to episodes of stress. There have been important conceptual advances, such as new ways to measure risk and price assets, and new insights into financial behaviour, through game theory and behavioural finance.

Yet we still have much to do in applying these insights to achieving the goal of a safe and efficient financial system. The task will be to develop mechanisms of supervisory oversight that make markets work better, not by suppressing the symptoms of market failure, but by addressing their causes. Setting financial standards that attempt to harness prudential instincts and deal with the underlying sources of market failure should play an important role in this endeavour.

4 COMPETITION, REGULATION AND FINANCIAL STABILITY[1]

Geoffrey Wood

Introduction

Financial stability is a curious concept. It is usually regarded as desirable, yet, like some other desirable things, it is believed to be hard to define. Some take the approach that it is obvious when we have it, while others define it by implied contrast with its opposite, a financial crisis. Unfortunately even that last course has problems, for while those who advocate it usually give a definition of a financial crisis, the definitions these various writers give are not all the same. In some cases they are very different indeed. One definition that has become classic – by which I mean that it has to be considered even by those who disagree with it – was provided by Anna Schwartz in 1986.

> A financial crisis is fuelled by fears that means of payment will be unobtainable at any price and, in a fractional reserve banking system, leads to a scramble for high-powered money ... In a futile attempt to restore reserves, the banks may call in loans, refuse to roll over existing loans, or resort to selling assets. No financial crisis has occurred in the United States since 1933, and none has occurred in the United Kingdom since 1866. (Schwartz, 1986: 11)

---

1   I am indebted to Charles Goodhart both for most helpful comments on a draft and for information on the history of currency boards, and to David Mayes for very useful discussions on the subject of this paper.

That definition is in a line which runs back to Henry Thornton, and to his 'Paper Credit' of 1802. It focuses on the banking system, and is concerned with the possibility that a bank failure would lead to a scramble for cash, which in turn can cause more bank failures, lead to a sharp contraction in the money stock, and then in turn to recession, perhaps even to depression. That chain of events is certainly not unknown; it is a brief sketch of what caused the Great Depression in the USA. The chain can be broken by the central bank acting as lender of last resort, and providing cash to the system so as to match the sudden, panic-driven, demand for it. Indeed, were it believed that the central bank would act in that way, there might be no panic-driven surges in the demand for cash. When urging the Bank of England to commit itself always to supplying cash in the event of a banking panic, Walter Bagehot argued along just those lines: 'What is wanted and what is necessary to stop a panic is to diffuse the impression that though money may be dear, still money is to be had. If people could really be convinced that they would have money ... most likely they would cease to run in such a herd-like way for money' (Bagehot, 1873: 64–5).

It is because the Bank of England has acted in that fashion when necessary ever since the crisis of 1866, and the Federal Reserve since 1933, that in Schwartz's view Britain and the USA have been free of financial crises since 1866 and 1933 respectively.

That definition of financial crisis, and of the procedure for dealing with it, have both in recent years been, if not criticised, then characterised as being due for sidelining. A broader definition should, it is often proposed, now be adopted.

In the first part of this essay it is argued that there is still a possible need for classic lender of last resort action. That done, the subsequent sections of the essay consider whether other actions may also from time to time be necessary.

Lender of last resort today

It is sometimes argued that now that capital markets are so much more widely developed than they were in the nineteenth century any solvent firm could get liquidity if it needed it. Further, it is suggested that significant flights to cash are also not at all likely to occur today – if people distrusted one financial institution they would just go to another that they did trust. The first of these propositions is not necessarily true in the absence of central bank liquidity provision; and the second is also not necessarily true.

Take as an example a computer failure; this could mean that the entire liquidity of the system was stuck in one place, or, say, that a bank's systems could receive but not make payments. There would be a sudden shortage of liquidity, just as in a classic banking panic, albeit for a different reason. In such an event, classic lender of last resort action – the injection of liquidity to meet a sudden temporary increase in demand for it – is still necessary.

And what about the claim that the financial system is nowadays so trusted that any institutional failure would be seen as an isolated event, while other institutions remained trusted? Is that really true? And is it true in every country? We know the answer to the second question: it is not. As for the first question, we certainly cannot be *sure* it is in any country. It would be a foolish central bank which gave up the classic lender of last resort role.

Fortunately few do so, although countries with currency boards rather than central banks can get into difficulties because currency boards are not always able to supply emergency liquidity on demand.[2]

The necessity of the classic role of the lender of last resort is not generally contentious; the dispute is, rather, about how often its function will be needed. Should that 'classic' role be extended? Some have argued that being a 'crisis manager' is part of that role. Fischer (1999), for example, maintains that by acting as a crisis manager the IMF has acted as an 'international lender of last resort'. It is not our purpose here to consider that 'international' version of the role of lender of last resort. But what is at issue is whether central banks should take on the role of 'crisis manager' to forestall events that could otherwise very well require them to act as classic lender of last resort, or, importantly, might be imperfectly resolvable even with such action.

This is clearly the way the Federal Reserve viewed its role in engineering the rescue of Long Term Capital Management (LTCM). Chairman Greenspan, in his Congressional testimony (1998: 1, 5), said, 'The act of unwinding LTCM's portfolio in a forced liquidation could not only have a significant distorting impact on market prices but also in the process could produce large losses, or worse, for a number of creditors and counterparties, and for other market participants who were not directly involved with LTCM ...' The creditors and counter-parties that the Federal Reserve was wor-

---

2   If the currency board has excess reserves above the required backing, such as were held by the Hong Kong monetary authority or the UK colonial currency boards, these can be used. Even if the currency board has no such reserves, so long as it or the ministry of finance can borrow reserves these can be used to back injections of liquidity. It is only when there are neither excess reserves nor the ability to borrow that lender of last resort lending is impossible; but such lending is always more circumscribed for a currency board than for a central bank proper.

ried about were big banks and securities firms, which might have been threatened by an LTCM default. By preventing the collapse of LTCM, the Federal Reserve may have avoided substantial problems at several large banks. In so doing, it saw itself forestalling problems, possibly substantial problems, at several large banks.

But there is actually a more persuasive justification than that for the Federal Reserve action (Edwards, 1999). In the LTCM episode the institutional mechanism for facilitating an orderly liquidation did not exist. Usually bankruptcy law provides for an automatic stay of the firm's assets. This prevents individual creditors from disposing of assets under their control and thus gaining an advantage over other creditors. LTCM's situation was different, and very special, because of its huge derivatives position. Derivatives contracts have statutory exception to the automatic stay provisions of the US bankruptcy code. They have clauses that give the counter-parties the right to terminate the contract in the event of a default *of any kind* by a counter-party. Further, in the event of such default and termination, counter-parties have the right to liquidate any of the defaulting counter-parties' assets that they have in their control, *even if the assets are not directly related to the derivatives contracts in question*. Thus, default by LTCM on any of its obligations would surely have triggered a 'run' by its derivatives counter-parties. The Federal Reserve in effect inserted itself as a trustee-in-bankruptcy where the law did not provide for one, and thus prevented the financial market turmoil that would otherwise have emerged from a legal lacuna.

There may, therefore, be a role for central banks in acting as crisis managers when the institutional mechanism or legal procedures are not in place for there to be an orderly liquidation of an institution and prompt valuation of its assets. Such circumstances may not be as unusual as one might expect on the basis of past experience, in view of the rapid liberalisation of financial markets around the world and the growing internationalisation of financial transactions. There are bound to be situations where the laws in one country conflict with those in another, and where the legal ambiguities are such that the liquidation of a financial transaction or institution may prove to be more difficult and time-consuming than expected, rather than as quick and orderly as is desirable.

But note that even such expansion of the role is intended to promote stability of monetary conditions. It is a new way, necessary because laws have not been adapted adequately to changes in financial markets, to achieve a long-established goal.

Redefinition of financial stability

Some writers have recently broadened the definition of financial stability well beyond that implied by the absence of a crisis as defined above. A very clear recent example is provided in the paper by Andrew Crockett in this volume. He maintains that financial stability involves maintaining the 'capacity of financial institutions and markets to efficiently mobilise savings ...'. Now, there are two separate and possibly quite distinct entities involved here – institutions and markets.

The argument for the importance of institutions can in part be traced to Bernanke (e.g. 1983) and his work on the Great Depression in the USA, and in part to the 'too big to fail' doctrine. Bernanke argued that the depth and length of the Great Depression could not be explained by the monetary contraction alone. It was, he suggested, also due in part to the number of banks that failed, leading to absence of 'channels of transmission' of credit from lenders to borrowers. This reduced investment and hence prolonged the recession. A puzzle with this theory is why the failed banks were not taken over, and run by new management with new shareholders; after all, that is what has often happened in more recent years when a bank has failed. The answer may well be that so many banks were failing, and the recession was so deep, that there was too much uncertainty for such takeover activity. The question must be, therefore, whether the results Bernanke found can support concern with institutions (as opposed to the classic lender of last resort concern with systems) in times less extreme than the Great Depression.

Can any bank be too big or too important to fail? Certainly in the nineteenth century the answer would have been no, as is well illustrated by the failure of Overend and Gurney. The consequences of that bank's failure were contained by classic lender of last resort action. In this context it is necessary only to note the vast (relative) size of that bank – by balance sheet ten times bigger than the next biggest. That historical episode does not help the 'too big to fail' doctrine.

What of Barings in 1890? Perhaps not too big to fail, but too important? Here, too, the 'too big to fail' doctrine does not get support. For before assistance was organised for Barings, efforts were made to find out whether or not the bank was solvent and whether its crisis was purely a shortage of liquidity. This was established by a rapid inspection of Barings' books. So an insolvent bank was not assisted. Since Barings was not insolvent, why could it not get assistance in the market? The answer to this is in two parts. Its assets were not sufficiently liquid to be discountable; and its shortage too great for any one bank to help by an unsecured loan. For the latter reason, a 'consortium' or 'lifeboat' was organised. Setting out fully why the Bank of England became involved in helping Barings would involve too long a digression. But the following points should be noted. Even then, the Bank of England, by being the bankers' bank, was seen as a custodian of the system. One of the Bank of England's responsibilities was ensuring convertibility of sterling into gold, and there were fears that the failure of Barings would trigger a foreign drain of gold. Finally, it should not be forgotten that the Bank of England was then still privately owned, had a commercial business, and was concerned that a major failure in London would damage this business.

In summary, nineteenth-century history provides no precedents to support 'too big to fail'. It is, however, now useful to consider what can be meant by 'fail'. Two aspects of the word must be clarified. As regards the first, it is true to say that in general large, well-diversified banks do not just collapse suddenly. Rather they decline, losing market share and perhaps shrinking absolutely as well as relatively. The problem we are dealing with is, so long as banks are allowed to grow and diversify, unlikely to be common. Nevertheless it is possible for a large bank, or group of banks, which comprises a substantial part of a country's banking system, to get into difficulties quickly. This happened with Finland's savings banks in 1992. Their problems were seen coming, but not by their management; so while something could have been done to contain the collapse, it was not. These institutions comprised in total some 30 per cent of Finland's banking system by balance sheet size; in terms of their share of the retail market they were larger than that. What can be done in such a case? Classic lender of last resort – the supplying of liquidity to the market – could undoubtedly have increased broad as well as narrow money. But would the remaining banks have had enough capital to allow adequate deposit expansion, and to compensate for the decline in velocity inevitable in such circumstances? Further, even had such expansion been possible, the efficacy of banks in transmitting funds from savers to borrowers could have been severely hampered, and with it the economy.

Even in such circumstances injecting capital so as to protect shareholders and failing management would be foolish; but liquidation of whatever assets there were, with subsequent closure, could very well be damaging to the economy. Here there can be a role for the central bank, a role properly described as that of crisis manager, certainly not properly described as that of lender of last resort. The central bank could act as an honest broker, finding a firm in the private sector willing to take over and run the failed institution, buying it for a token sum, injecting new capital, and supplying competent management. That was exactly how the Bank of England behaved when Barings failed in 1995.

Alternatively, if such a buyer cannot be found sufficiently promptly to keep the institution running, and if it is important that it be kept running without even a brief pause, then the central bank can organise a public sector purchase and capital provision, and run the organisation until a private sector buyer can be found or a gradual run-down can take place. (Keeping the bank running in the public sector for an indefinite period should be out of the question for a long and varied list of reasons.)

To summarise on this point, the troubled institution (or set of institutions) is allowed to 'fail', in the sense that shareholders lose wealth and the management jobs; but the business is not liquidated or closed. This leaves unsettled the issue of what should happen to depositors. Should they lose as well as shareholders? The answer surely must be that they should be protected to the extent of whatever deposit protection was in place before the failure, and no further; otherwise, what was the point of the deposit protection scheme or its absence?

Now it is necessary to pause at this point and look back at the nineteenth century. After all, as observed above, when Overend and Gurney failed in 1866, it was a huge bank relative to the rest of the system – bigger by that comparison than any bank today. No problems occurred as a consequence of not keeping it running; what problems there were resulted from the Bank of England being tardy in acting as lender of last resort. Why did no problems arise from the bank's closure? One can conjecture that this was a result of the network of bank interdependencies being less extensive than it is now; but that is only conjecture, for no work has been done to test that hypothesis. Accordingly, while the case for keeping an institution running (as described above) is persuasive, it lacks the strong empirical backing that would be provided by demonstration of what has changed between 1866 and now to make such action necessary.

A second possible reason for 'crisis management' action would be if a set of well-run banks were suddenly affected by a common and unforeseeable shock. It is hard to conceive of one consistent with the survival of society which would cause the overnight collapse of banks such as Britain's clearing banks; but should such an event occur, action that is appropriate at the time should be taken. The best way to prevent that statement being vacuous is by example. An imperfect example – imperfect because even then problems were not on that scale – is the effect of the outbreak of war in 1914 on the London money markets. Seabourne's account of this (1986), 'The Summer of 1914', gives a splendid description and analysis of how these problems were handled.

An argument for bailing out insolvent banks sometimes heard is that in a time of crisis it is hard, perhaps impossible, to tell an illiquid from an insolvent bank. Accordingly, a central bank should simply decide whether or not it wishes to lend to a bank, and not concern itself with the bank's solvency. Bagehot's (1873) advice was to the contrary; in a crisis, 'advances should be made on all good banking securities and as largely as the public ask for them' (p. 70). This advice, Goodhart (1999) observed, was '... to distinguish, in part, between those loans on which the central bank might expect, with some considerable probability, to make a loss (bad bills and collateral) and those on which little, or no, loss should eventuate' (p. 351). That is surely right. But Bagehot's advice was also intended to serve another purpose. Showing that there is nothing new in the insolvency/illiquidity argument, Ralph Hawtrey (1932) tackled it with his characteristic lucidity:

> In the evolution of the Bank of England as the lender of last resort, we have seen how at the beginning it was inclined to ration credit by refusing all applications in excess of a quota, but later on its restriction took the form of limiting the kind of security it would take. It is not ordinarily possible to examine in detail the entire assets of an applicant for a loan. Demonstration of solvency therefore cannot be made an express condition of the loan, at any rate at a time when the need for cash has become urgent. But the furnishing of security makes scrutiny of the general solvency of the borrower unnecessary. The secured debt being covered by assets more than equivalent to it, there is less need to enquire whether the remainder of the borrower's assets will be sufficient to cover the remainder of his debts. (pp. 126–7)

Hawtrey goes on to elaborate how the type of security accepted should be broadened in a crisis, and, while doing so, again implies that the purpose of taking security is to make irrelevant the solvency of the institution that seeks to borrow: 'The right course is rather to accept any security representing a sufficient amount of wealth to cover the loan with adequate margin, without being too particular in defining the form of the security or even in insisting on its immediate marketability' (p. 130).

The case for taking collateral is clear and strong. Nevertheless, one can perhaps imagine circumstances in which a well-run bank is hit by a shock, one no fault of its own and which it could with sufficient liquidity survive, but for which it has insufficient collateral for the amount of liquidity required. It has obtained all it can from the market, but needs more. What should the central bank do then? Manifestly, it could first lower the standard of collateral it will accept. If that should not prove sufficient, one might start to have doubts about the troubled bank being well run; but be that as it may, there might conceivably, if these doubts are stilled, be a case for very short-term unsecured lending. It cannot be emphasised enough, however, that this case depends on a sequence of events, every one of them in itself unusual, occurring one after another; and even then the case is not overwhelming.

What is the role of the central bank in preserving the efficiency of markets in their role of transmitting savings? Here we need to distinguish between the 'mechanical' trading system and the liquidity it needs to function. The central bank can supply the latter; when it should is discussed below, under the heading 'Asset prices'. If the former suffers mechanical failure, presumably its owners will fix it; and if the organisation threatens to become insolvent, then its operations can be continued while shareholders and management suffer, as described earlier.

So there is justification for adding the management of some

kinds of crisis, in addition to the traditional lender of last resort facility, to the list of a central bank's responsibilities. But surely Andrew Crockett (see the chapter by Crockett in this volume) goes too far when he suggests that the 1992 collapse of the ERM was a crisis. After all, what happened afterwards? In Britain, for example, there was a prolonged low-inflation recovery, producing steady growth and falling unemployment for almost the subsequent ten years. It was really rather like what happened in 1931, when Britain left the gold standard – an event that was (in Schumpeter's words) greeted with a 'sigh of relief', and was followed by a long inflation-free economic upswing. In both cases it was the *defence* of the currency which came very close to causing a crisis: the abandoning of the defence, after a turbulent few days, averted the crisis.

The enlarged role of the financial sector in the economy

Do we need to worry more about financial stability, and expand regulation and official intervention, because finance now plays a bigger role in the economy; because, in other words, there is so much more financial intermediation relative to national income than in the recent past? Here it is important to retain some historical perspective. The increased financial intermediation that we see is not a break with past history, but a continuation of a long-running trend. This is shown in the work of Raymond Goldsmith (e.g. 1985). The financial intermediation ratios he calculates, for a range of countries, have all been rising for about as long as he was able to accumulate data – not steadily, of course, but fluctuating about a rising trend. Thus the problems, if any, of increasing financial intermediation are developments of what we have seen in the past – and we can learn from the past.

A lesson from the past

Central banks – for example, the Bank of England – have, in many cases, two responsibilities nowadays. These are financial stability and monetary stability. What is the connection between them? How should we expect long-term price predictability to affect financial stability? We should not perhaps expect price stability to deliver perfect financial stability as a by-product, but it should certainly make it easier to attain as it both reduces rate volatility at every point in the yield curve[3] and facilitates assessment of credit and interest rate risk. Does the evidence support this conjecture? We can look at evidence from the years of the gold standard to see.

It is a little difficult to make direct and straightforward comparisons between the gold standard era and the present day, for the behaviour of prices then was somewhat different from now. The trend was flatter; indeed, in Britain (and in the 'gold standard' part of the world overall) prices drifted down from 1870 to the mid-1890s, and drifted up thereafter until 1914. On average over the period, the price level ended up essentially steady; this is quite different from now, when the price level rises steadily, albeit more slowly than it has done in the recent past. The short term, too, is different, for prices sometimes rose and fell quite sharply year by year. Nevertheless, that is the period which comes closest to the present in terms of long-run price-level behaviour.

Britain and the USA had very similar price experience, but very different financial stability experience. In the gold standard period the British banking system was very stable, while that of the USA

---

3   It has this effect all along the yield curve because policy rates are stable at the short end, and long-term rates are not pushed around by changing inflation expectations.

experienced a stream of failures. Why? Two factors were crucial – the lender of last resort and the difference between good and bad regulation. Britain had in the Bank of England an effective lender of last resort from 1866. This provided stability in the banking system; hence the absence of crises since that date which Schwartz (1986) noted. The USA, in contrast, did not have a central bank until 1914, and even then it did not act consistently in that role until after the Great Depression. That is well known. What is also well known, but perhaps less often noted in this context, is the effect regulation has on banking structure. In Britain banks were allowed to merge, and to diversify both geographically and by activity. In the USA, in contrast, geographical diversification was restricted, and unit banking close to being the norm. The system was thus failure prone, and failures were common. Two points follow. First, while financial stability benefits from price stability, other factors matter. Second, we have a clear demonstration that regulation can impede financial stability. Regulation needs to be designed carefully. A more recent example of the same point is provided by Japan. In the aftermath of the collapse of asset prices there, the Japanese banking system was very weak, and so in turn was the Japanese economy. This resulted because the banks had been allowed to count the appreciated assets in their capital – so when asset prices collapsed, so did their capital. Bad banking to do it, and bad regulation to allow it.

Asset prices

Mention of asset prices leads to a consideration of whether central banks should concern themselves with asset prices and, if so, why and how. Should central banks target or stabilise them?

A useful start here is to pose two questions. Would we think it prudent if central banks started to use monetary policy to control house prices? Surely not. More generally, suppose there is a boom in asset prices generally, including in equity prices. If the boom were based on a rational assessment of improved future prospects, we would surely not want it stopped. And if it really were irrational, could monetary policy stop it?

This is not to say that central banks should not monitor asset prices for any information they may give about the future behaviour of the economy. That is a different matter altogether. Note, too, that it is legitimate to intervene if the problem is a sudden shortage of liquidity. Indeed, that is a traditional central banking role. It was carried out well by, for example, the US Federal Reserve in 1987, when it injected liquidity when trading was drying up because of a lack of it; and then withdrew it before it had any undesired inflationary consequences.

This recommendation may suggest an asymmetric response to asset price fluctuations – ignore booms, but provide liquidity if trading dries up because of lack of liquidity during an asset price slump. This is how the US Federal Reserve has behaved in some episodes (October 1987, as noted above, and also October 1988, and 2001); and it has been criticised for doing so. There have been two criticisms. First is the claim that it has led to the 'Greenspan put' – the claim that in effect the Fed is underpinning the market. This would seem a little unfair, for the aim of the policy is to facilitate trading rather than stabilise prices. (The first may of course contribute to the second – or not.) Discussing that criticism would be a diversion from the subject of this paper, but discussing the other criticism is not.

The second criticism is as follows. Asset price rises when they become 'unsustainable', and certainly, when they are large, generate a probability, maybe very small, of a sharp reversal. If central banks are concerned to avoid worst-case outcomes, then they should worry about 'bubbles' because of the risk of subsequent 'bursts'. Although undoubtedly persuasive, is this argument convincing? There must on balance be doubts. First, the evidence that asset price crashes cause, precipitate or predict recessions is not compelling (Wood, 2000). Second, any harmful consequences that might occur if markets seized up in consequence of the collapse are prevented by liquidity injection if needed. Third, the record of central banks when tightening monetary policy because they are worried about a 'bubble' is not encouraging; on more than one occasion their doing so has produced a sharp downturn in the real economy. All in all, the balance seems to be that the preferable policy – perhaps only because it is the lesser of two evils – is to let asset price booms run their course but ensure that there is sufficient liquidity in any ensuing price crash.

Standards and codes

Central banks acting collectively have in recent years set, promulgated and helped to implement standards – of capital ratios and so forth – and codes of good banking practice on an international basis (see also Howard Davies's paper in this volume). This is to an extent good, but there is a risk that it becomes bad. The good lies in the fact that it helps countries with emerging capital markets and banking systems quickly to reach a standard that means that other banking systems feel safe when dealing with them. This facilitates international mobility of capital and helps make the banking systems themselves more stable.

There are, however, two dangers. The first is that there is, as noted above, good and bad regulation. Which is which? To some extent – but only to some extent – we know. Surely, therefore, there is an advantage in encouraging diversity in regulatory regimes, so that competition between them serves a discovery process similar to that which it serves in normal markets. There would not be a 'rush to the bottom' – a rush to the regime with least restrictions, regardless of any other qualities. Banks are no more enthusiastic about 'going broke' through dealing with unreliable counterparties than are any other businesses. That is the positive reason for encouraging regulatory competition. There is also a negative reason. If the rules are the same everywhere, then when problems arise everyone may behave in the same way – and this could well be destabilising. For example, it has been argued that in the late 1990s and the early part of the 21st century, insurers in the UK all felt under pressure to sell equities at the same time because of the 'resilience test' that formed part of the UK regulatory regime.

Conclusions

Discipline of firms is in general left to the financial markets and to the law. Why do we treat firms that provide financial products and services differently? In particular, why is market discipline seen as insufficient to preserve financial stability? Key to the traditional answer is that in modern economies there is a monopoly supplier of liquidity. Hence, as well as market discipline to enforce prudent individual behaviour, we need a lender of last resort to preserve system stability against the kind of shocks that are possible even when every individual member of the system is behaving well. The resulting problem, as was recognised by Thomson Hankey (at various times in the mid to late nineteenth century Governor, Deputy Governor or a director of the Bank of England), is what is now called moral hazard. Further, because banks need capital as well as liquidity, and the central bank can supply only the latter, regulation may be needed to internalise the externality that failure by an insufficiently capitalised bank would cause. There is a case for good regulation.

How do we know what is good as opposed to what is bad? One cannot simply say that bad regulation will not be implemented; it has been in the past – note, for example, restrictions on bank branching in the USA. So can we lay down any general principles? One principle is provided by the distinction between prescriptive and proscriptive regulation. The former says what must be done; the latter says only what cannot be done. The former prevents innovation by the discovery process of competition; the latter does not. Hence the former impedes economic progress; an example of this is that among East Asian countries similar in most respects except their framework of regulation, those with proscriptive frameworks have prospered greatly compared to those with prescriptive frameworks.

Perhaps even more important in the present context, proscriptive regulation makes it much more likely that different institutions will do different things to preserve their own strength and thus, when shocks come, different members of the financial system will respond in various and different ways, not all tending in the same direction. That is important – for even if the action taken were in the right direction, all institutions doing the same things together might cause problems.

But even the best regulation may not prevent all problems, and these problems may not always be of the type calling for the remedy of classic lender of last resort action. When such problems arise, they may, as discussed above, require the central bank to act as crisis manager. This is quite different from the lender of last resort function, and could sometimes be carried out by an institution which, unlike the central bank, is not able to supply liquidity. But with its knowledge of the monetary and banking systems, the central bank is likely to be the most appropriate institution to carry out such a crisis management function. Its tasks could involve ensuring the prompt and orderly takeover of a failed important group of institutions; the injection of liquidity to prevent financial markets drying up; acting when legal frameworks are inadequate for private sector resolution of some problem; and (when times are calm) advising on, and urging, the creation of legal frameworks appropriate and adequate for such tasks. But all this is a change of emphasis, not a revolution. The increasing complexity of the financial system may have changed the balance between the roles a central bank has to fulfil, but it has not yet necessitated the assumption by it of any role that would have been either new or objectionable to the two great nineteenth-century expositors of the art of central banking, Henry Thornton and Walter Bagehot.

References

Bagehot, W. (1873), *Lombard Street*, John Murray, London (reissued by Wiley, Chichester, 1999).

Bernanke, B. (1983), 'Non-monetary effects of the financial crises in the propagation of the Great Depression', *American Economic Review*, vol. 73, no. 3 (June): 257–76.

Edwards, F. (1999), 'Hedge funds and the collapse of long term capital management', *Journal of Economic Perspectives* 13 (spring): 189–210.

Fischer, S. (1999), 'On the need for an international lender of last resort', *Journal of Economic Perspectives*, vol. 13, no. 4 (autumn): 85–107.

Goldsmith, R. W. (1985), *Comparative National Balance Sheets: A study of twenty countries, 1688–1978*, University of Chicago Press, Chicago.

Goodhart, C. (1999), 'Some myths about the lender of last resort', *International Finance*, vol. 2, no. 3 (November): 339–60.

Hawtrey, R. (1932), *The Art of Central Banking*, Longman, Green and Co., London.

Schwartz, A. J. (1986), 'Real and pseudo financial crises', in F. H. Capie and G. E. Wood (eds), *Financial Crises and the World Banking System*, Macmillan, London.

Seabourne, T. (1986), 'The summer of 1914', in F. H. Capie and G. E. Wood (eds), *Financial Crises and the World Banking System*, Macmillan, London.

Wood, G. E. (2000), 'The lender of last resort reconsidered', *Journal of Financial Services Research*, vol. 18, no. 2/3 (December): 203–28.

5 MANAGING FINANCIAL CRISES
Warwick Lightfoot

Introduction

Until the 1980s, the issues of bank runs, deflation and asset price bubbles as discussed in texts such as Charles Kindleberger's book *Manias, Panics and Crashes: A History of Financial Crises* (Kindleberger, 1978) may not have seemed that relevant. Certainly, until the middle of the 1990s the main preoccupation was to bring inflation under control, to manage the process of disinflation and to revitalise market economies by making greater use of the price mechanism. In that context asset price bubbles, bank runs and systemic financial crises seemed to be matters for economic historians rather than for policy-makers in central banks and government departments. However, from the middle of the 1980s onwards, the issues discussed by Kindleberger came to be of importance again, in a number of countries: both for policy-makers and for practitioners in financial markets.

There were serious concerns about Third World debt and the deterioration of the balance sheets of big international banks in the 1980s. The savings and loan crises in the USA followed; and there was the collapse of equity markets in October 1987, with the concerns that collapse stimulated about potential adverse wealth effects on investment and consumption. The failure of Barings in 1995 neatly brought things full circle. A great banking house rescued by the Bank of England a century before returned to knock at the door once again.

The 1990s saw all the central concerns raised by Kindleberger and new dimensions to financial crises played out in the Mexican, Asian and Russian crises. The collapse of Long Term Capital Management was a dramatic event and a compelling illustration of the way novel sources of risk from derivatives could destroy a balance sheet. It also illustrated that complicated financial problems and mismanagement of risk are not confined to transition economies and emerging markets nor to firms that lack sophisticated expertise. These problems can arise closer to home and in institutions in which intellect and technical expertise are readily available.

In this chapter, we begin by looking at the sources of financial crises and the appropriate regulatory response to them. The relationship between the tax system and the financial system is shown to be an important factor in weakening corporate governance, thus contributing to problems in financial markets.

Stable prices and the credit cycle

It was commonly thought twenty years ago that, if the advanced economies returned to a rough approximation of price stability, financial markets would also probably be more stable (see also the chapters by Crockett and Wood in this volume). With hindsight such thinking could be regarded as naive. It neglected to take full account of the role of capital markets in allocating resources and the relative price effects that one might expect to see, and it failed to pay enough attention to the credit cycle identified by bankers and economists more than a century ago. Victorian and Edwardian Britain and America enjoyed genuine price stability yet exhibited dramatic credit cycles and asset price bubbles in the context of that price stability. Returning to approximate price stability has been a very important achievement, but on its own it is not a guarantee of a world in which asset price bubbles and banking failure that carries potential systemic risk are either eliminated or minimised. Avoiding inflationary and deflationary monetary shocks nonetheless makes a significant contribution to transparent and efficient financial markets, and low and stable inflation should help to stabilise money and capital markets.

The relationship between macroeconomics and microeconomics

There is now much greater recognition of the connections between macroeconomic and microeconomic issues. A good example is the labour market. Unemployment is an important aggregate variable and a central macroeconomic policy objective. Ensuring that there is sufficient aggregate monetary demand to maintain high levels of employment is widely accepted as important across the spectrum of economic opinion. But the need for flexible labour market institutions and the critical role of microeconomic issues in determining structural unemployment are now recognised as well.

Bank lending, foreign exchange movements and bond and equity prices are normally considered in relation to developments in macroeconomics (central bank interest rates, monetary conditions and so on). However, these variables also respond to relative price changes and changes in relative demand and supply. Asset price bubbles and excessive bank lending leading to a deterioration in corporate and household balance sheets are less likely to take place in an open and competitive market environment. An environment where prices can adjust to changing supply and demand and where information is transparent and transaction costs are light will not eliminate speculative bubbles but will contribute to avoiding a framework of incentives that leads to such bubbles. Most asset price bubbles are stimulated or at least aggravated by a perverse set of incentives that prevents markets from working in an efficient way.

A legal framework and proper regulation

Market economies cannot work without proper social and legal institutions. Property rights and contracts cannot be enforced without effective and efficient legal remedies. In many respects this is obvious. It was something recognised by Adam Smith, and it is something that has been exemplified by the practical difficulties of the former communist transition economies since 1989.

Financial markets need specific frameworks of regulation and supervision to ensure transparency and appropriate standards of behaviour by parties to a transaction. Market participants have long recognised this. Organised marketplaces and stock markets emerged because people wishing to transact business found it convenient to do so in a setting where rules were laid down and enforced. Transparent access to information is central to the efficient operation of financial markets. Most people would now accept that efficient, transparent, liquid financial markets amount to a public good the benefits of which are felt beyond the narrow confines of participants in certain self-regulated financial markets. That is the case for systematic government intervention to establish a reliable framework of regulation for the operation of financial markets and financial services in general. The difficult question is to know how far regulators should go in trying to protect the public. The Gower Report in 1984 played an important part in moving financial market regulation from a framework of privately arranged self-regulation to a more systematic framework based on statute and the application of the concept of public interest to financial regulation. Professor Gower (1984/85) wrote that regulation 'should not seek to achieve the impossible task of protecting fools from their folly', but instead should aim to be 'no greater than is necessary to protect reasonable people from being made fools of'.

The essential rationale for the regulation and supervision of banks is the damage that can be generated to confidence in the system as a whole by the collapse of one bank. Bank failure has the potential for disastrous consequences that are of a fundamentally different character and order from the damage done by the collapse of a large corporation or the contraction of an industry. In practice this means that the authorities cannot allow banks to fail, given the wider impact such events could have on the financial system and the economy as a whole. This does not mean that every bank in trouble needs to be rescued, but the practical recognition that in many cases a large bank would be bailed out creates a climate of moral hazard. That moral hazard is at the heart of the justification for the extensive supervision and regulation to which banks are subject in most sophisticated economies. In effect regulation is the price that banks pay for potentially having a lender of last resort. Without proper supervision, an environment distinguished by bank rescue rather than bank failure would lead to reckless lending in the knowledge that the wider community and ultimately the taxpayer would pick up the bill for such imprudence.

Traditionally the systemic risk was usually thought to be

principally associated with if not confined to banks. It is, however, increasingly clear (see the chapter by Davies in this volume) that such crises can arise in firms that would not in any normal way be categorised as banks. Such firms might include investment funds trading in derivatives, insurance companies, commodity trading houses and what one might regard as straightforward utility or gas and oil supply corporations trading in derivatives and developing new tradable futures products. This tends to be regarded as a recent phenomenon, but whether it is genuinely novel is less clear. The US legislation setting out the eligibility criteria for institutions that could access the Federal Reserve system's discount windows, passed in the 1930s, for example, was very broadly drawn. As well as providing credit for banks, the criteria were intended to accommodate commerce, industry and agriculture by providing emergency lending to individuals, partnerships and corporations.

The Basel Accord

In recent years there have been no financial crises in which the confidence in financial institutions or markets generally has been lost or where there has been an actual or serious risk of collapse of the whole financial system. Individual institutions and sectors have created genuine problems and great difficulties for the individuals involved, but there has not been a systemic financial crisis. An important reason for this has been the success of the Basel Accord on capital adequacy which came into effect in 1988. It has played a crucial role in ensuring that bank balance sheets are much stronger than they were twenty years ago. But significant risks may not have been eliminated but rather transferred off the balance sheets of banks. The use of devices such as securitisation and the creation of credit derivatives have enabled banks to pass these risks on to other entities such as insurance companies. Nonetheless the banking system appears to be much better capitalised for the risks with which it is dealing than it was in the early 1980s.

Financial crises stimulate regulation

Asset price bubbles burst, and when they do, as Adam Smith himself suggested, we can get 'overtrading, followed by revulsion and discredit'. From the time of the South Sea Bubble, financial crises have often been followed by implementation of new financial regulation. These bouts of legislative activity have not always been examples of well-targeted intervention, and they have often had long-standing adverse consequences. For example, legislation has prohibited activities and arrangements that can be beneficial or created perverse incentives and imposed unnecessary and damaging costs on an economy.

The Great Depression of the 1930s provides good examples of regulation that conferred little additional benefit at the cost of preventing banks from achieving economies of scale and diversification. The Economic Report of the US Council of Economic Advisers in 2003 lucidly sets out some of the issues involved. The 1934 Glass-Steagall Act was passed as a response to the conflicts of interest that potentially occur when banks have better information than investors in securities and bank depositors. When inherently risky investment banking activities involved in issuing securities are combined with commercial banking the principal danger is that banks may be tempted to use their superior information to take advantage of less well-informed depositors or investors. Depositors could be harmed if in the absence of deposit insurance banks engaged in risky transactions resulting in them holding poorly performing and risky assets on their balance sheets, without an increase in their equity capital to protect bank depositors from losses. Deposit insurance effectively transfers these risks to the insurers. The risks to depositors can also be reduced through the application of minimum capital reserves.

The historical evidence suggested that in the 1920s, before the new regulations were introduced, banks had higher capital-to-asset ratios than afterwards. Moreover, in the 1920s investors found that so-called universal banks that conducted both investment banking and commercial banking were effectively penalised by those entering into contracts with them: in other words the market responded to the potential information asymmetry in the way it priced contracts. Securities underwritten by such banks had to offer higher yields given the conflict of interest that was recognised by the market. In order to avoid being penalised in this manner banks created separately capitalised investment banks with their own balance sheets and separate boards of directors. In fact the quality of securities issued by integrated banks did not differ from that of the securities issued by specialist investment banks, and there is evidence that integrated banks benefited from economies of scale arising out of the use of common resources, assets and knowledge. The Glass-Steagall Act is a good example of ill-conceived and potentially costly regulation imposed after a financial crisis. It also provides an illustration of how enduring such legislation can be. That act was passed in 1934 and was not finally repealed until Congress passed the Financial Services Modernisation Act, more commonly known as the Gramm-Leach Bliley Act, in 1999.

The Basel Accord imposed international regulation to ensure that banks engaged in international lending were properly capitalised for the risks that they were taking. It was an agreed response to the Third World debt crises and the impact these crises had on bank balance sheets. It was also designed to ensure that banks operating in markets away from their home supervisors could not 'shop around' until they found supervisors abroad who were conveniently relaxed about capital adequacy. It has in many respects been a success. However, it also provides practical illustrations of the way in which regulation can offer perverse incentives for financial institutions to engage in so-called regulatory arbitrage. Banks take opportunities to substitute government deposit insurance or public capital for private capital. The accord had the great merit of being easy to administer, and the tension between regulators seeking to deter excessive risk-taking and banks that seek ways around inefficient or simply uneconomic regulations is not new. But the Basel Accord provided a clear illustration of that tension, and a concern to remedy its defects lies at the heart of the attempts to agree a second version of the accord.

The experience of the Basel Accord also provides an example of how technical and regulatory changes to bank capital ratios can have significant implications for monetary conditions and macroeconomic policy. Reducing and liberalising prudential minimum reserve requirements have often been associated with an expansion of bank lending and a loosening of monetary conditions. An obvious example of this was the expansion of bank lending and broad money associated with the reduction of minimum reserve requirements as part of the Competition and Credit Control reform introduced in the UK in 1971. The application of stiffer capital adequacy rules for banks in the early 1990s was associated with a tightening in monetary conditions and a reduction in bank lending throughout the OECD. While it was not the only factor at work, the consequences of the Basel Accord probably compounded other disinflationary measures being taken by national monetary authorities in individual countries, but most notably in the USA and the UK. This is a good illustration of the way in which something that might principally be thought of as a microeconomic issue, namely bank regulation, has macroeconomic consequences.

The microeconomic sources of asset price bubbles

There is a vast literature on the relationship between monetary policy and the misalignment of asset prices. Yet there has been less work done attempting to understand the connections between microeconomic policy measures and asset prices. In 2001, the G10 finance ministers and central bank governors asked for work to be done exploring these issues, and the Bank for International Settlements published a paper (BIS, 2003) in response to this request for more information. The paper examines how in the context of greater price stability there has not been greater financial stability. It draws attention to the way in which incentive structures, taxation and regulation can contribute to asset price bubbles and their sudden deflation. Poor timing in the implementation of otherwise beneficial programmes of financial deregulation was a feature of asset price bubbles in advanced OECD economies in the 1980s. Liberalisation of regulation, combined with inflation and powerful tax incentives, led to a build-up of asset prices. Then measures to cap the inflating bubble were introduced too late and too abruptly, and also at a time when economic conditions were deteriorating. Defaults and bankruptcies often followed falls in asset prices.

Price stability clearly limits the risk of excessive asset price movements in a number of ways. It reduces volatility in the rate of inflation; it removes the risk of rapid falls in inflation which tend to increase the value of outstanding debt in an unexpected manner and increase the likelihood of defaults; and it removes the distortion of asset prices that can lead to excessive borrowing to acquire assets as well as to a broader misallocation of resources. Yet even with a return to approximate price stability, problems with financial stability still exist. Big movements in asset prices are often unrelated or only weakly related to changes in fundamental value. When asset prices rise sharply this is often associated with an increase in the ratio of the asset price to the conventional measure of its current fundamental value. For example, strong equity prices are accompanied by high price–earnings ratios and the ratio of property prices to rents rises.

Moreover, when the values of assets return to more normal levels relative to fundamental value, this is usually as a result of a fall in prices rather than an increase in fundamental value. This indicates that market expectations were not realised. For example, equity markets return to lower price–earnings ratios as a result of falling prices rather than from earnings increasing.

A genuine improvement in fundamental value appears to stimulate overly optimistic expectations about the future. Such optimism raises asset prices, a process that can be further reinforced by the herd instincts that have been identified as a feature of financial market speculation for two hundred years or more. This process stimulates a price correction and more normal historic valuations assert themselves.

In recent years genuine improvements in the supply side of economies and lower inflation have led to an improvement in the split between real and nominal growth in money GDP. These real improvements have sometimes resulted in overly optimistic decisions which are then disappointed. The structure of microeconomic incentives in many countries either helps to stimulate such asset price bubbles or can aggravate them.

The financial sector has had a structure of incentives that encourages excessive risk-taking. This appears to apply both to individual lending officers and entire financial institutions. The impact of the Basel Accord on monetary conditions in the early 1990s has been referred to in the context of the unintended consequences of regulation. The accord has also been identified by some people as a potential source of pro-cyclical vulnerability in advanced economies. This arises from the fact that capital requirements are risk-based. This means that banks need to hold more capital at exactly the time when capital is scarce – that is, when economies are entering recessions and credit losses are rising. If banks change their lending policies over the cycle there will be a further adverse consequence, with over-optimism during periods of expansion, which leads to an accumulation of bad loans in the following period of contraction. Such a process is illustrated by the experience of Japan in the late 1980s and early 1990s, and there is also evidence that comparable problems affected Sweden in the early 1990s. In both instances banks allowed people to borrow against collateral provided by rising asset prices, and that credit was then used to further invest in the same asset.

When banking regulation is liberalised and interest rate ceilings, lending limits, guidance on lending priorities, barriers to entry and exchange control are either relaxed or removed, there is a powerful response. Banks are very competitive in the new environment and are determined to acquire market share. If there have been quantitative limits on the total level of bank lending there is likely to be pent-up demand for loans from both households and corporations. This is probably aggravated if quantitative limits on loans have been compounded by the uses to which credit is put. Deregulation can lead to a surge in credit growth. This credit is then used to purchase assets that are in relatively fixed supply, resulting in asset price inflation. This process is powerfully reinforced when there are favourable tax arrangements for investment in fixed assets.

The timing of aspects of deregulation appears to be important. A good example is provided by the decision of Sweden to deregulate its banking system while retaining foreign exchange controls and barriers to entry. A surge in credit was invested in a limited supply of domestic assets because, when these became expensive, there were no other assets in which investors could invest: exchange controls prevented them from investing in foreign markets that might have offered better fundamental value.

Tax policy also has an important impact on asset prices and can be highly distorting. In many tax regimes there is a bias towards debt finance at the expense of equity capital. The cost of servicing debt is tax-deductible for a corporation, while the costs of servicing equity are not. Returns to equity capital are generally taxed at the corporation tax rate, dividends are then further taxed in some regimes, and capital gains, arising from retained profits that have already been taxed, may be taxed again. A firm can increase its after-tax returns by increasing debt and reducing the tax wedge on its earnings. The higher the marginal tax rate the greater the incentive to engage in leverage. Such leveraging of balance sheets increases the risk of default, aggravates volatility of share prices and exposes equity prices to shifts in the tax regime.

In many countries households can deduct interest payments in full, and many forms of investment income are taxed at lower rates, but these lower rates do not apply to (already taxed) equity investments.

There are often biases towards certain classes of assets in tax regimes. Home ownership is widely promoted. Mortgage interest payments are tax deductible while the capital gain and imputed rental income are untaxed or less than fully taxed. When property ownership receives a tax subsidy and marginal income tax rates are both high and steeply progressive, and also capital gains tax rates are relatively low compared with income tax rates, there are powerful drivers that will raise asset prices. The UK, Sweden and the Netherlands provide good illustrations of this over the last 30 years.

What this illustrates is that while asset price cycles will never be eliminated, regulation and taxation should be designed to avoid aggravating them. The requirements appear to be ensuring that the timing of deregulation is right; preventing the potential perverse consequences of partial deregulation; and the need for a coherent and neutral tax system.

Lender of last resort function

The role of a lender of last resort has been recognised as crucial for the avoidance of systemic financial crises since the time of Bagehot – indeed, perhaps before him, from the time of Thornton. How that function can be discharged without the creation of systematic moral hazard is difficult to determine. It is also difficult to know how to apply Bagehot's rubric of lending to illiquid but not insolvent institutions (see also the chapter by Wood in this volume). In the context of securitisation, marked to market valuations and the development by banks of complex derivative positions, distinguishing insolvency from illiquidity is probably harder now than it once was. It is certainly the case that economists and supervisors working in the US Federal Reserve system recognise this as an issue in the context of federal legislation on deposit insurance and giving banks access to the discount window.

The home of the concept of lender of last resort is London, and the institution that pioneered the function in the nineteenth century was the Bank of England. Perhaps during the twentieth century, particularly in the 1970s and 1980s, it became too ready to play that role when the circumstances did not really require it. In the 1980s many money market practitioners were content to place money on deposit with the traditional merchant banks, the so-called accepting houses, in the confident belief that the Bank of England would never let an accepting house go under. This tendency to be too ready to be a lender of last resort was best illustrated by the rescue of Johnson Matthey. As a bank it was of little significance, and the Bank of England was mainly concerned about the consequences the failure might have had for the gold bullion market, because the bank's parent company was a significant dealer. The Bank of England rescued it, which was probably an example of being too willing to undertake the role of lender of last resort, when the danger of systemic risk was remote. The episode damaged the reputation of the Bank of England and stimulated interest in removing its banking supervision function, which eventually happened in 1997.

The Bundesbank, in contrast, always stressed that it did not see itself as a lender of last resort. This was because it was determined to avoid encouraging moral hazard, although in practice it would have to facilitate that function when a genuine systemic problem arose. But it was probably an appropriate fiction to maintain, given that it provided some degree of ambiguity about a lender of last resort being available to help out reckless and imprudent institutions. The fact that the Bank of England did not rescue Barings for a second time in 1995, and allowed that famous bank to go under, has probably gone some way to correct the impression given in the Johnson Matthey case. The decision to let Barings go was a useful demonstration that imprudent institutions in the UK would not automatically be rescued from their own folly.

An international lender of last resort?

The Mexican, Asian and Russian crises in recent years have stimulated interest in the potential need for an international lender of last resort. This is an understandable response to the dramatic events in the individual countries, and it is reasonable to ask whether the various crises would have been less acute if the international financial community had known that there was an identifiable and reliable lender of last resort such as the International Monetary Fund (IMF).

Whether an international lender of last resort would have helped, or whether it might have aggravated a difficult position, depends on how one views the crises involved. If the problems were essentially those of short-term illiquidity, but where clearly beneficial projects would yield long-term social and private returns in excess of their costs, a lender of last resort of the sort envisaged by some people might have been a help. If, however, the problems arose out of fundamentally ill-conceived public policy that distorted money and capital markets and led to a misallocation of resources and losses of economic welfare, a lender of last resort would have made matters worse rather than better. Given that these crises involved poor banking regulation, a lack of transparency, unusual relationships between governments and corporations, deficient structures of corporate governance and imperfect legal institutions for dealing with insolvency and bankruptcy, further compounded by brittle fixed-parity foreign exchange regimes, it is not clear that an international lender of last resort would have been helpful. Indeed, the experience of generous lending to Mexico and Russia raises awkward questions about moral hazard rather than opening up a clear international agenda for introducing such a lender of last resort. There should at least remain a high degree of ambiguity about the availability of such a lender. While Bagehot, in his book *Lombard Street*,[1] is the most famous formulator of the concept, he himself was very cautious about its merits and concerned about its potential for damage. Giving the resources and the explicit role of lender of last resort to a body such as the IMF would run the danger of removing the desirable ambiguity that ought to surround the concept when it works at its best, should such an international lender actually be found to be desirable.

Corporate governance, rent seeking and the divorce of ownership from control

A distinguishing feature of the Asian crises in the late 1990s was the lack of transparency in capital markets and deficient structures of corporate governance. Since the onset of the bear market

---

1   W. Bagehot, *Lombard Street*, John Murray, 1873, reissued by Wiley, 1999.

in equities it has become plain that there are also genuine issues of transparency and corporate governance in the advanced economies of the OECD. The behaviour of equity analysts,[2] the conflicts of interest highlighted by Eliot Spitzer, the New York State Attorney General, and the extraordinary episode of Enron are striking examples of abuse.

Yet leaving aside these egregious examples of abuse there is a broader agenda of economic agency problems and rent seeking that needs to be tackled. In many respects it is more difficult to identify effective measures that would remedy the problem. The heart of the problem is the divorce between the ownership and the management of capital. The executives and directors of corporations effectively manage and control other people's capital. As a result of this effective control, they are well placed to pursue their own agenda. This may involve goal displacement, such as replacing the principal objective of the shareholder maximising the rate of return on capital with other corporate goals, such as expanding balance sheets or partaking in expensive but not very profitable projects or activities that interest the management. This goal displacement may be much cruder, such as putting the pay and remuneration of managers ahead of the returns paid to shareholders.

In the past large corporate headquarters, staff leisure facilities and management projects that were expensive and added little to shareholder value exemplified such goal displacement. Over the last ten years the character of goal displacement appears to have changed. Managers have been keen to demonstrate that they are cutting fat out of the bottom line. Many of the elaborate headquarters buildings and suchlike have gone. Instead there appear to be

---

2   See also Congdon (2003).

examples of management organising corporate balance sheets to maximise their own rewards. Executive pay has been a focus of public attention and comment. The more striking examples of this form of goal displacement have been where managers use shareholders' money not to pay dividends but to engage in the purchase of the corporation's own shares. The purpose of this can be to drive up the value of the shares to maximise the value of the share options that management staff hold as part of their compensation packages.

These issues of protecting investors from the rapacious hands of company directors and managers who may not be acting principally in the interests of their shareholders are at the heart of the issues raised in the economic theorists' discussions regarding the divorce of the ownership and management of capital. These issues were first raised in the 1930s, when institutional shareholding began to be widespread. And in recent years they have taken on a lurid character that few people would have expected. Finding appropriate remedies for tackling these issues will be difficult. One of the interesting features emerging from the debate on the double taxation of dividends in the USA is the way in which a tax regime that penalises the distribution of earnings through dividends encourages corporate goal displacement and the kind of behaviour that policy-makers would normally try to curb. A more neutral tax system that mitigated the double taxation of savings held in the form of equity is a worthwhile objective in its own right. It may also be one way of curbing such corporate behaviour by changing the pattern of incentives that managers face. However, tax reform of this nature would not alone fully resolve the broad problems that are apparent in corporate governance: it may have to be accepted that there is no complete solution to this problem.

Conclusion

There is much greater macroeconomic stability amongst OECD countries than there was during the 1960s, 1970s and 1980s. However, this does not necessarily prevent financial crises, whether widely or narrowly defined, from happening. The sources of financial crises can be microeconomic in nature. A legal framework and appropriate regulation are, of course, important to ensure confidence in financial markets. However, there are forms of regulation that can create moral hazard and which have arisen in response to financial crises and have often had adverse consequences. The microeconomic sources of financial bubbles and banking crises have often manifested themselves because of inappropriate timing or an incomplete process of financial deregulation. For example, the liberalisation of a banking system whilst exchange controls are still in place has caused undesirable results, as in the Swedish banking crisis. A lender of last resort function is important, but it is also important that it is used sparingly and that there is ambiguity about the circumstances in which it will be used. The relationship between the tax system and the financial system is important. There are many aspects of the tax system in OECD countries which make financial crises more likely and contribute to the problem of poor corporate governance.

References

Bagehot, W. (1873), *Lombard Street*, John Murray, London (reissued by Wiley, Chichester, 1999).

BIS (2003), *Turbulence in Asset Markets: Role of Micro Policies*, Report of the Contact Group of the Bank for International Settlements, Basel, Switzerland.

Congdon, T. (2003), 'Resolving Conflicts of Interest in the Financial System', *Economic Affairs*, vol. 23, no. 1.

Gower, L. C. B. (1984/85), 'Review of Investor Protection', Cmnd 9125, HMSO, London.

Kindleberger, C. (1978), *Manias, Panics and Crashes: a History of Financial Crises*, Basic Books, New York.

6 CREATING AN INTEGRATED EUROPEAN MARKET FOR FINANCIAL SERVICES
Alexandre Lamfalussy

The context of the moves for European financial market reform

The Committee of Wise Men on the Regulation of European Securities Markets has developed a programme for regulatory reform. However, in the light of recent events in financial markets in general, and in the USA in particular, we should ask whether we are still as sure as we were three years ago that the development of liquid, transparent, innovative, well-integrated – and therefore efficient – European financial markets should be a priority policy objective. The conclusion to which this chapter will come is 'yes'. But we must draw the lessons from these past three years' experience.

It is worthwhile recalling the state of mind of most of those involved in the discussions on regulatory reform in the late 1990s, when the broad objective of European financial market integration was firmly put on the policy-makers' agenda, which then led to the launching of the Financial Services Action Plan (FSAP) and at a later stage to the mandate given to the Committee of Wise Men to review the regulatory process prevailing in the securities markets. One strong motivation was that the single market could not become a reality, and therefore yield the expected dividends, without it being extended to cover the market for financial services. It was also felt that EMU was about to lift a major non-tariff barrier to the exchange of goods and services, which raised the expectation of an upsurge in cross-border financial flows inside the euro zone.

In addition, the US example was influential. By that time it had become obvious that there had been a marked upward shift in the rate of growth of US labour productivity – the size of this is still debatable, but not the fact itself. More generally, the growth performance of the US economy, with fast productivity increases going hand in hand with job creation and declining inflation, was regarded with admiration. A widespread belief took hold that the efficiency of US financial markets in general, and of equity markets in particular, played a major role in achieving these results. It did so by generating innovative financial instruments and techniques, by responding to the needs of surging entrepreneurial initiatives, by diversifying the range of products available to savers – in short, by improving the allocation of resources. Much of this was supported by an impressive flow of academic research.

This widely accepted view spilled over into more specific manifestations of admiration of the 'American model' which were perhaps less generally shared but still attracted a growing audience. The market-centric nature of the US financial system was given high marks in comparison with the bank-centric European system of financial intermediation. The seemingly endless bull market and the resulting extraordinarily high rate of return on equity investment were attributed to the high (actual and expected) profitability of US firms, which in turn was thought to be stimulated by the efficiency of US corporate governance, including the incentives provided by stock options.

By contrast, many Europeans were deploring the lack, or the excessively slow development, of an 'equity culture' in continental Europe, the only slowly emerging interest of management in 'value creation', the inability of European corporations to make swift policy decisions in response to the challenges raised by globalisation, and the low level of profitability of many European corporations in comparison with their US competitors.

There were signs of change in Europe. Stock options were beginning to be considered as part of normal management incentive schemes. A number of corporations decided to set themselves the target of raising return on equity. Traditional stock exchanges were being challenged by 'new markets'. Thousands of Internet companies were set up in most European countries. But all this was still far from even beginning to bridge the gap between the 'US model' and European reality. Moreover, the performance of Europe's 'real' economy continued to lag well behind that of the USA. Hence the insistence on speeding up the implementation of the Financial Services Action Plan and reforming the creaking European regulatory process with the explicit objective of enhancing, via integration, the efficiency of European financial markets.

Recent events in the USA

It is worthwhile considering where we are now in comparison with, say, the autumn of 1999. A number of things have happened during this time which, in the eyes of many, raise doubts about the wisdom of putting the financial integration process so firmly at the top of the European policy agenda. Few financial market participants would share these doubts – and I do not either. Nor do I perceive any signs that our political leaders, the Commission and Euro MPs are having second thoughts about the initiatives taken some time ago. As a matter of fact the implementation of the FSAP is proceeding reasonably well within the framework provided by the new four-level regulatory process. But it would be foolish to ignore the growing disenchantment of wider public opinion with the working of financial markets and with many of the arguments that have been put forward in favour of creating an integrated financial services market in Europe.

What has gone wrong during the past three years? There are three interconnected groups of events: the collapse of the equity market bubbles; the loss of confidence in corporate governance, corporate reporting and, more generally, the checks and balances supposed to ensure a smooth, fair and efficient working of financial markets; and the large-scale misallocation of resources revealed by the boom-and-bust cycle.

We have now had three years of a bear market. This has amounted, roughly speaking, to halving the broad stock market valuations in comparison with their peak values – somewhat less in the USA and more in some European countries. In those sectors that were supposed to be the driving force behind the so-called 'new economy' the collapse of equity prices has been significantly more than 50 per cent on both sides of the Atlantic. I do not have to dwell on what this has implied for those life assurers that invested heavily in equities, or for pension funds and, via these funds, for corporate liabilities. All this is well known. But regarding Europe, consider two issues. One is that, as a result of the recent public interest in equity investment (often stimulated by privatisations), the share of newcomers in households' equity portfolios has been substantial. These newcomers derive no consolation from the fact that those who started buying equities before the mid-1990s have still registered positive rates of return until now. The second issue is the political impact of these developments on the ongoing debate about how to reform our pension systems: this is potentially disastrous.

Is loss of trust an essentially US phenomenon? Given the large numbers of 'Enrons' in North America, and the numerous examples of outright criminal behaviour, it is often argued that this problem is more serious in the USA than in Europe. This may be true to some extent, but not entirely. There are many examples in Europe of high-tech companies that had been regarded as textbook cases of entrepreneurial success (which was well reflected in their capitalisation), the bankruptcy of which has led to criminal proceedings, although the main cause of most of the European 'horror stories' is probably mismanagement rather than criminal misbehaviour. But I am not convinced that those who lost 90 per cent of their investment regard this distinction as very relevant. Investors lost their trust not only in corporate management but also in the functioning of internal and external audit, in the behaviour of investment banks, in the investment advice given by financial analysts, and even in the trustworthiness of the legal profession or the professional capability of the supervisory authorities.

The third piece of bad news has been the truly monumental misallocation of resources that has been revealed during the past three years – a misallocation that found its origins in the exuberant or 'extrapolative' expectations formed during the boom years. Some examples of this resource misallocation are worth highlighting. The Internet boom is the most striking example. A very large proportion of the Internet ventures, which had attracted tens of thousands of talented and enterprising young people and led to sizeable ITC investment, went bust. Some of these were very large enterprises. Recently the largest-ever loss in US corporate history was announced.

The degree of indebtedness of a number of prestigious telecom companies reached stratospheric levels, reflecting excess investment, large-scale acquisitions and purchases of third-generation licences. The sale of mobile telephone handsets has not collapsed, but investment in network equipment has. Moreover, beyond these industries, we witnessed a genuine merger and takeover mania motivated by over-optimistic evaluations of synergies and the easier financing facilities provided by the bull market. A large proportion of these mergers and acquisitions have turned out to be genuine failures, which is now prompting a global revision of corporate strategies back to 'core activity'. With the appearance of ample excess capacities in large segments of both manufacturing and service industries, cost cutting and lay-offs have become the central preoccupation of management. And so the difficult question arises as to how human, financial and physical resource misallocation on such a large scale can be reconciled with the basic proposition that well-functioning financial markets lead to a better allocation of resources. This also happened at a time when financial markets, in particular in the USA but also in a less spectacular way in Europe, were becoming more rather than less innovative, more rather than less competitive, more rather than less liquid, when the flow of information was improving rather than deteriorating: in short, when markets were becoming more rather than less efficient both in the commonsense meaning of the word and in the sense given to it by economists.

The impact of recent corporate events

These events should not lead us to fundamentally revise the views held some three years ago regarding the major contribution to growth we could expect from financial market integration in Europe; but these views should be qualified by our recent experience. Let me expand on this. A useful starting point is to recall two facts that support a relatively optimistic stance.

The first is about the course taken by US labour productivity. We now know that some of the initial estimates regarding the pick-up of productivity growth in the second half of the 1990s were exaggerated. But even with a downward adjustment there can be no doubt that there was a quantum jump in the rate of growth of labour productivity from the mid-1960s onwards. Moreover, productivity has continued to grow during the past three years (and quite spectacularly in 2002), which is an unusual experience in a recessionary or a slowing economy, auguring well for further growth.

The second fact is that despite the equity bear market, Enron and 11 September, the financial system of the developed world, and notably that of the USA, has not been driven into a genuine financial crisis. This is partly due to Basel I, which was instrumental in allowing banks to enter the period of turbulence with a strong capital base. Most banks' capital in 1999/2000 was well above the minimum requirements, which suggests that bank management had adopted on the whole a cautious policy stance; but there is no doubt that the regulatory-driven Basel I initiative played a major role in shaping the attitude of management. A number of banks also made ample use of credit derivatives in unloading a substantial proportion of their credit risks on willing risk-takers. Given that banks still retain their key position as providers of liquidity and as major players in the payments system, the global effect of this redistribution has very likely been a positive one from the point of view of systemic stability, even though the cost for institutional investors has been substantial: the same point applies to the rising share of bond financing in corporations' total debt. Last but not least, credit should be given to the swift and radical interest rate cuts in the USA undertaken by the Fed, which among other influences allowed consumer spending to sustain the US economy. This will be discussed further below.

What about the nasty experience of dysfunction in the world of corporations? It is important, but we should keep a sense of proportion. Listening to some sections of the media, one gets the impression that there has been collective misbehaviour among all corporations, especially in the USA, but perhaps also in Europe: this, of course, is not true. What remains true, however, is that there have been enough cases of dysfunction to warrant serious action, such as revision of accounting standards, reforms of corporate governance and dealing with conflicts of interest.

Regulatory responses to recent market events

But how should we proceed to ensure that the appropriate reforms take place? Some oppose spontaneous market-led reforms to regulations. There are other chapters within this volume, as well as elsewhere in the literature, considering this issue on a priori grounds.[1] This chapter is not the place to cover these issues in detail. In a number of instances, regulation by competent authorities is unavoidable, but even in these instances market participants and all interested parties should be given the opportunity of having their voice heard. The key point is that any such consultation should start before embarking on a legislative process and should

---

1   See, for example, *Economic Affairs*, vol. 23, no. 3, 2003.

continue when it comes to writing out the specifics of implementation. This takes time but, given the complexity of the issues at stake, we should take our time. Taking speedy action when the stories of misbehaviour are still unfolding may be thought to be politically rewarding, but the end result will be poor-quality regulation and legislation.

There is an absolute necessity for multilateral agreements when it comes to accounting standards, and for broad agreement, at least within the EU, on issues of corporate governance and conflicts of interest. The USA taking speedy and tough legislative action without seriously consulting anybody is regrettable. European governments should not revise their company laws, nor should their regulators develop new corporate rules of behaviour, without systematic consultation.

We also have to try to understand what lies behind the multiplication of instances of corporate dysfunction. The answer is quite simple: the long period of economic upswing combined with the exuberance of equity markets. One could not imagine Enron or Vivendi happening in an environment in which the main equity price indices were increasing on average by 5 to 10 per cent. The uncomfortable conclusion is that, while reforming accounting rules, improving corporate governance and eliminating obvious conflicts of interest are worthy objectives to be pursued in any event, we should harbour no illusions: even much improved rules will be overcome by the deleterious effects of the kind of equity market bubbles that we experienced during the last years of the 1990s.

Policy lessons from recent experience of market turbulence

The contribution of well-functioning financial markets to growth cannot be assessed other than by looking across cycles. It is important to take into account the following points: business cycles and their corollary of financial exuberance followed by financial distress have been, and remain, integral to the working of capitalist market economies; cycles are part and parcel of the adjustment mechanism that corrects the misallocation of resources generated during boom periods; the longer and the more violent the periods of exuberance, the more likely the build-up of unsustainable financial imbalances and the emergence of large-scale resource misallocation – and, therefore, the more painful the unavoidable correction; whilst it would be neither feasible nor indeed desirable to 'abolish' the business cycle, there are good reasons for trying to moderate its excesses; one of the key questions we should ask ourselves is whether financial globalisation aggravates, or on the contrary alleviates, the propensity of our system to produce asset price cycles or short-term volatility.

I do not know the answer to this last question, and my suspicion is that the jury will remain out on this issue for quite some time. The question is addressed, to some extent, in the chapter by Crockett within this volume. We would certainly be well advised to look carefully into the policy challenges raised by this issue. It is worth noting that our Committee of Wise Men said in its final report two years ago:

> while the Committee strongly believes that large, deep,
> liquid and innovative financial markets will result in
> substantial efficiency gains and will therefore bring
> individual benefits to European citizens, it also believes

that greater efficiency does not necessarily go hand in hand with enhanced stability ... Increased integration of securities markets entails more interconnection between financial intermediaries on a crossborder basis, increasing their exposure to common shocks ... Given the growing interlinkages between all segments of the securities markets and the full range of financial intermediaries, the Committee believes that there is an urgent need to strengthen co-operation at the European level between financial market regulators and the institutions in charge of micro and macro prudential supervision.

We said this in our final report despite the fact that one of the few parts of our initial report that triggered adverse comment, by some weighty market participants, had referred to the potential risk of increased asset price volatility. It was politely but firmly suggested that we drop the subject.

In the remainder of this chapter, two broad courses of action that policy-makers could take to alleviate the financial hardships caused by the boom-and-bust sequence will be considered – the purpose of such action should be to moderate the consequences of this sequence rather than to try to suppress them. The first course of action relates to the regulation of solvency of financial institutions, reform of which in essence (though not necessarily in all its practicalities) is receiving broad support. To a very large extent necessary reform, in response to recent events, relates to bank regulation and supervision – more specifically increasing the crisis-resistance capability of banks and keeping a rein on their crisis-generating proclivities. But why concentrate on bank-ing rather than on the whole range of financial intermediaries? Is it not true that there has been a blurring of demarcation lines between traditional commercial banking and other financial intermediaries? And do we not observe the declining importance of banking intermediation relative to the role played by market transactions? These points are valid but, despite these developments, banks have so far continued to play a central part in the potential emergence of a systemic crisis as much as in its prevention. Via their deposit base and credit-granting activities, they are the providers of liquidity to the system: it is through the banks that the central bank's ultimate liquidity creation affects other financial intermediaries as well as the real economy. In addition, they play a key role in the payments mechanism, which is *the* channel through which specific crisis manifestations are liable to develop into a full-blown general crisis.

It is worth commenting further on two issues that have a bearing on bank supervision and regulation at present. The first is about Basel II, which is supposed to replace Basel I in the not too distant future. For reasons that are well known, Basel I, which made a major contribution to preserving systemic stability, has outlived its usefulness. There seems to be broad agreement on the basic philosophy of Basel II and on a host of specifics as well. But there are serious concerns about the potentially pro-cyclical impact of Basel II. When all major banks use similar risk assessment methods, and when all of them apply these methods at the same time in the presence of similar adverse developments, and when marking to market is universally practised, pro-cyclical developments seem to be likely to occur. But it is important to note that not everyone shares this view.

The second issue is the role of central banks in bank supervision and regulation. The issue has arisen in connection with the extension of the four-level approach proposed by the Committee of Wise Men on the Regulation of European Securities Markets to the banking industry – indeed, to the whole of the financial industry – the implementation of which is under active discussion. I am broadly sympathetic to this initiative, if only because I cannot see how Basel II could effectively be implemented in Europe (and after the implementation swiftly adjusted to changing market circumstances) without making a clear distinction between the first three levels. But I have some concerns about the way in which the role of central banks is handled. The issue is not whether central banks should or should not act as bank regulators and supervisors. It is accepted that in some European countries central banks act in this capacity, while in others they do not. The issue is about the place given in the new regulatory and supervisory structure to those European System of Central Bank (ESCB) members that fall into the second category and, by implication, about the place given to the European Central Bank (ECB).

There is no disagreement on the crucial part to be played by all ESCB members, and therefore by the governing council of the ECB, in crisis management. Everyone agrees that when there are accumulating signs of an impending crisis, two courses of action have to be taken as a matter of priority. One is to pump central bank liquidity into the banking system; the other is to ensure the smooth functioning of the payments system. The primary responsibility for undertaking these actions lies with the Governing Council of the ECB. But, in addition to general liquidity creation, crisis management may have to entail specific actions aimed at preventing the collapse of individual institutions. In some instances bail-outs will have to imply the actual (or potential) use of public money and at that stage the primary responsibility for running these operations will have to shift to governments. The demarcation line between general liquidity creation and bail-outs that commit taxpayers' money will in most cases be fuzzy – crisis management will always be a messy business – hence the absolute necessity for well-designed procedures for communication and cooperation between central banks and governments.

It would seem advisable to involve all central banks in crisis prevention arrangements, for two reasons. One is that it is very difficult to define where crisis prevention stops and crisis management begins. It is also hard to make any operationally clear distinction between micro and macro prudential concerns. We badly need cross-fertilisation among all institutional players.

Satisfactory prudential arrangements coupled with prompt and skilful liquidity creation by central banks are likely to diminish the risk of a full-blown systemic crisis and therefore eliminate the most dramatic consequences of an equity market 'bust'. But such success will not come without a price. This price is moral hazard. And that price may be high, even if both governments and central banks make it clear that their crisis-fighting commitment is in favour of the system rather than specific institutions: the 'system', unfortunately, is the sum total of specific institutions. If we are going to use policy instruments to moderate the 'bust' and create moral hazard, it leads to the question of whether we therefore need to moderate the boom. The boom may be moderated anyway, to some extent, if bank regulations are designed in a way that tends to rein in the banks' inclinations to abandon caution and prudence when things appear to be going well. For instance, mandatory – and very demanding – stress testing may go in the right direction. But this may not be enough because banks' risk-taking activity cannot be regarded as being the dominant, and certainly not the exclusive, factor in the development of asset price bubbles. Hence we need to look for other ways and means of trying to moderate manifestations of exuberance, and quite specifically the emergence and persistence of asset price bubbles.

In the wake of the 1987 Wall Street meltdown we saw the proliferation of inquiries into investment and trading techniques which may have played a part in creating excessive asset price – mainly equity price – volatility. This research, which still continues, has not yielded convincing and widely accepted conclusions. In any event, there are legitimate doubts about the possibility, indeed the desirability, of trying to regulate such techniques with the objective of limiting their volatility-creating effects. The main reason for these doubts is that most of these techniques provide risk-averse market participants with hedging devices, and by tinkering with them one could destroy their hedging capabilities.

Should we assign monetary policy the duty of trying to moderate asset price bubbles? Central bankers' reluctance to accept such an assignment is well known and understandable. Two main arguments are put forward. First, equity price levels, let alone real estate prices, cannot be 'targeted', for unlike the rate of inflation (as measured by the rate of increase in the retail price index) there can be no meaningful discussion about the 'right' level of asset prices. Second, the transmission mechanism of monetary policy in the direction of asset prices is, to say the least, uncertain – and there is a genuine risk of recessionary 'over-kill' if monetary policy is used to 'burst' asset price 'bubbles'. There is also the 'political' argument that, while targeting price stability may receive broad popular support, it would seem hard to muster popular support for deflating excessive asset prices.[2]

2   See Goodhart in M. Friedman and C. A. E. Goodhart, *Money, Inflation and the Constitutional Position of the Central Bank*, IEA Readings 57, Institute of Economic

While all this is eminently reasonable, the problem remains: asset price bubbles do have nasty consequences, as anyone can see today. Could or should central banks try to rein in the market's proclivity towards irrational exuberance? It may be argued that the reappearance of over-optimism akin to that which we saw at the end of the last century is unlikely to become a major concern in the short run. Perhaps this is exactly the right time to consider this matter carefully.

Affairs, London, 2003, for a discussion of this issue and of other authors' views on the issue.

7   COMPETITION IN FINANCIAL REGULATION

Philip Booth

Introduction

Currently, there is increasing pressure for the international harmonisation of financial regulation. This pressure comes from a number of different sources. There is pressure on corporations to produce accounts that accord with internationally set standards. The debate on fair value accounting for UK pension schemes and the implementation of FRS17, for example, has arisen from international pressure for fair value accounting; there is a parallel move towards fair value standards to be applied in the banking and insurance sectors (see, for example, Hairs et al., 2002, for a discussion of fair value accounting in the insurance sector). Pressure for internationally recognised minimum capital standards for banks that trade internationally gave rise to the Basel I accord and the proposed Basel II accord which develop common capital adequacy standards across national boundaries. There is pressure for harmonisation of regulation across the EU in the area of securities markets and financial services: see, for example, European Commission (2000) and Howard Davies's, Adam Ridley's and Alexandre Lamfalussy's papers in this volume.

These moves towards harmonisation do not have a common origin. It is possible that moves towards more uniform accounting standards can arise through market pressure without any direct intervention by government or regulatory authorities.[1] Investors or creditors may wish to be able to judge different companies, particularly those that are traded or quoted on an international basis, using the same 'measuring rod'. Harmonisation can arise as a result of national governments acting independently of each other or as a result of action taken by supra-national organisations such as the EU. In some areas, such as banking regulation, there may be a genuine and possibly even well-founded belief that an inadequately regulated bank in one jurisdiction may fail, leading to 'contagion' through the payments system so that banks which are sound and regulated in other jurisdictions fail too. Harmonisation of regulation may or may not be an appropriate response to this perceived problem. Nevertheless, an economic case for such harmonisation could be made[2] and the subject of banking regulation will not be considered further.[3]

The main focus of this paper will be the regulation of non-bank financial intermediaries (particularly insurance companies, although the points made are relevant to pensions funds too). In this case, the main economic justification for regulation is consumer protection. The following argument is used in favour of regulation of non-bank financial institutions: there are information asymmetries between producer and consumer; it is expensive for consumers to find out about the solvency positions of different providers of financial services; regulation is therefore justified to ensure that all providers meet particular standards. In fact, this

---

1   The author is not saying that market pressure alone is the reason for the harmonisation of accounting standards, merely that such a situation is possible.

2   The author would argue that the case for harmonisation is a weak one. The different banking activities in different countries could be regulated separately.

3   This subject is discussed in more detail in the papers by Geoffrey Wood and Andrew Crockett in this volume.

problem can be addressed through the market, without government regulation (see Booth, 2003). However, where regulation does exist, this paper argues that there is no reason to harmonise such regulation across different legal jurisdictions within any area that is attempting to remove barriers to trade. Uniform regulation is not necessary to facilitate free trade. Mutual recognition of regulation across jurisdictions is a preferable way to facilitate free trade in financial services.

What is meant by harmonisation and mutual recognition?

Harmonisation of regulation can be defined as the development of common regulatory principles, laws and rules across jurisdictions. Harmonisation contrasts with mutual recognition. In the latter, practices and principles recognised within one jurisdiction are recognised within others. For example, under mutual recognition, a French insurance company could trade in the UK, regulated by the French authorities, even though French regulation might be different from UK regulation. The UK authorities 'recognise' French regulation and, in turn, the French authorities 'recognise' UK regulation. It is also possible not to have any international co-operation on regulation so that, in the above example, a French insurance company would have to set up a UK subsidiary, regulated under UK law. Free trade would still be possible even under such a regime, and this is discussed below.

Mutual recognition and harmonisation are not mutually exclusive. For example, in the EU, in non-bank financial services markets, 'mutual recognition' of regulation is the norm. Nevertheless, there is a minimum degree of harmonised regulation. Even here, however, the harmonisation that has taken place has been sufficient to 'fossilise' insurance regulation and institutionalise practices that belong in a different age (see below).

Free trade and harmonisation

Is harmonisation of regulation necessary for free trade? If it is not necessary, then the practical obstacles to developing harmonised regulatory systems considered in Adam Ridley's paper in this volume, together with the theoretical reasons for preferring mutual recognition, would suggest that international harmonisation of regulation, in non-bank financial services, is a goal that policy-makers should not seek to achieve. Before considering this question, it should be noted that the goal of free trade is not necessarily the same goal as that of a single market (see also below). While the UK governments of the 1980s and 1990s thought that the phrases 'single market' and 'free trade within the EU' could be used inter-changeably, others believed that the term single market had wider connotations. Harmonisation of regulation might be proposed not to facilitate free trade but to facilitate a deeper but possibly related process of political union.

The EU is not the first entity to consider the relationship between free trade and deeper economic and political relationships. The USA faced the same question in its own development. Bollick (1994) draws some parallels that are useful. Article One, Section 8 of the US Constitution gives Congress the right to regulate inter-state commerce. The intention of that article was to prevent impediments to trade being developed by individual states. It is also worth mentioning that the ninth and tenth amendments of the US Constitution were specifically designed to protect the rights of states and individuals against encroachment from federal government. They allowed states and the people to retain all freedoms, unless action was specifically provided for in the Constitution at a federal level.

Some analysts point to these safeguards and note that the encroachment of US federal government on the activities of states and the people was not prevented even by these, quite specific, constitutional clauses; therefore there are concerns about the more limited safeguards inherent in the principle of subsidiarity in the Maastricht Treaty. This issue will not be considered further.

Nevertheless, it is notable that, in many respects, a greater variety of regulatory frameworks and regulations is tolerated in many areas of business in the USA than is the case in the EU, despite over 200 years of US federalism. Insurance regulation was only relatively recently harmonised across states and then only partially. Harmonised regulation, it appears, is not a precondition for federation, and thus is clearly not a pre-condition for free trade or free inter-state commerce. Harmonisation of regulation can give rise to greater transparency and reduced search costs by customers who would be faced with products regulated under a single regime. But if harmonisation is not a pre-condition for free trade, one should also consider the very significant disadvantages of harmonisation of regulation.

It should be mentioned that it is not sufficient merely to point to one example of a federation that has not considered harmonisation necessary to demonstrate that harmonisation is not, indeed, a necessary condition for free trade. It is possible, though not likely, that the regulatory system in the USA is an impediment to trade but that political pressures have prevented harmonisation. It is therefore worth exploring the relationship between harmonisation and free trade further. An analogy could be drawn with rugby (see also the paper by Ridley in this volume which uses a similar analogy). There are three codes of rugby: American football, rugby union and rugby league. The rules of these codes could be harmonised to ensure that rugby players in all countries could play in all other countries. But why merge three codes of rugby? Why deal with the technical detail and difficulties of that approach? Why remove the competitive process by which each code of rugby can develop optimal regulations? Free trade in rugby services to spectators could be achieved simply by allowing different teams to come into different grounds playing under their different codes. Consumers can choose between the codes. There would be no single code of rugby or harmonisation of rugby regulation but there would be free trade and consumer choice. In each rugby ground, there would be mutual recognition of the validity of the different rugby codes. All that would be necessary would be for two teams to agree to play to the same set of rules.

Similarly, under mutual recognition of financial regulation, all that is necessary is for two trading entities (an individual and a corporation or two corporations) to agree a contract regulated by the same regime. There could be a number of different recognised regulating entities in a single market. Indeed, those regulating entities would not all have to relate to particular national boundaries. In the rugby example, two regulating entities exist within the UK (rugby league and rugby union) and the same regulating entities exist within France: regulation does not follow national boundaries but there is still competition between regulators. The rugby example is, of course, an example of the evolution of private regulatory systems.

It is also worth noting that, at one level, there is no real difference in the approach that needs to be applied to manufactured products and that which needs to be applied to services. All products, even simple retailed manufactured products, come as complex, differentiated bundles of services. This insight reflects a mature understanding of the realities of markets which is sometimes lost in neo-classical models of perfect competition (for a critique of such models see, for example, Kirzner, 1992). However, in the case of financial services regulation there is an additional complexity that has made the debate more complicated and the creation of a single market more difficult. With most services, and also with manufactured products, a service that is sold is generally subject to regulation in the country in which it is sold (even if such regulation amounts only to basic law requiring the fulfilment of contracts). All that is necessary for free trade is non-discriminatory treatment of products with different origins. In fact harmonisation of rules in relation to such products and services does occur in the EU. However, such harmonisation is not necessary for free trade, although it might increase the opportunity for economies of scale (if they exist) among producers.

With regard to financial services, an aspect of product quality is the solvency of the institution that sells the product. This helps determine the risk of the product. Therefore, regulators in a country into which a product is sold have an interest in the regulatory framework in the country from which it is sold. Thus the issue of regulation can become intertwined with debates regarding free trade. But as long as regulators are satisfied that consumers understand that there are different regulatory environments in which products from different countries of origin can arise, mutual recognition is still sufficient for free trade.

Harmonisation, mutual recognition and the single market in insurance services

In non-bank financial services, helpful distinctions have been made between different types of trade. We can think of the development of free trade at three different levels. First, trade can arise through the capital markets. A company in any one EU country can be allowed to purchase a financial services company in any other country or set up a subsidiary in any other country. The entity would be regulated in the country in which it was active. This happens freely in the EU. For example, a French company, Axa, owns a number of UK brands and, indeed, there are complex cross-holdings of shares in Axa involving individuals and companies in a number of EU countries. There are no substantive policy issues here. Free trade already takes place at this level. Neither mutual recognition nor harmonisation of regulation is necessary. Each insurer is regulated in each country in which it does business. However, arguably there are greater frictional costs from relying on this mechanism for facilitating free trade. Subsidiaries have to be set up in any country in which an insurer wishes to do business. But no international cooperation on regulation is necessary to establish free trade in this way. All that is necessary is for each government to remove impediments to foreign nationals setting up subsidiaries.

At a further level, free trade can be developed through the mechanism described by the EU as 'freedom of services'. As an example, take two countries such as the UK and Holland. A UK company can sell services into Holland to Dutch people but with no physical presence. The company is then regulated under UK law. The idea behind allowing freedom of services was that it was felt that it would only be wholesale players who understood the market well who would actually purchase products across borders under freedom of services. Such players did not need so much regulatory protection and therefore no minimum level of EU regulation would be necessary.

Finally, there is the principle of 'freedom of establishment' which forms the basis of the third life insurance directive. Under this principle a company in a country such as the UK can set up a branch in another country, such as Holland, but regulated by the UK supervisor. It is here that the debate on regulatory approaches takes place. It is argued by some that one needs the maximum amount of harmonisation in order to create transparency and a genuine single market in services. However, the so-called mutual recognition approach has been taken instead. There is a relatively light level of harmonised regulation but, under freedom of establishment, a company from country X can establish in country Y, under country X's regulations, which may be different from those of country Y. According to a recent PricewaterhouseCoopers/ Financial Services Ireland survey, freedom of establishment is of relatively small importance in comparison with freedom of services where financial services are traded: see Daly (2003). It is freedom of services or the full-scale establishment of subsidiaries which facilitates most trade.[4]

In relation to insurance the treaties establishing the European Communities have been clear from the beginning that 'Restrictions on the freedom of establishment of nationals of a member state in the territory of another member state shall be abolished by

---

4   It should be noted that the debate on regulation relates to the prudential regulation of institutions. The consumer protection regulation or product regulation of the country in which a product is sold always applies, no matter where a company that sells a product is established: see also below.

progressive stages … Such progressive abolition shall also apply to restrictions on the setting up of agencies, branches or subsidiaries by nationals of any member state established in the territory of any member state' (Article 52 of the Treaties Establishing the European Communities).

This objective has been progressively achieved, particularly by the implementation of the first and third non-life and life directives, the third directives dating from 1992. The third directives required countries to accept the principle of freedom of establishment based on mutual recognition and required little more harmonisation of insurance regulation than had previously occurred. Pressure for a harmonised, illiberal framework of regulation was resisted. Indeed, one of the main features of the agreements surrounding the implementation of the third non-life and life directives was that the range of regulation that states were allowed to impose was limited, as such regulation (for example, that requiring product approval) might inhibit competition and trade. Thus far, free trade has been developed in the insurance market through mutual recognition.

Regulatory change

There are forces driving regulatory change in the insurance markets. It has generally been recognised that those harmonised regulations which do exist in the EU are out of date. Indeed, this author would argue that they are so out of date, yet so fundamental to the provision of information to the marketplace that takes place through the regulator, that they encourage bad practice and the provision of misleading information. Currently, there is a review of regulation taking place. It is still intended in the EU insurance company solvency requirements review process (Solvency II) that harmonisation will be at a relatively low level of regulation, but it is quite likely that more sophisticated, risk-based capital requirements will be brought in for insurers. However, even here the EU may require only adherence to a set of principles with detail being determined at national level (see, for example, Creedon, 2002, for an outline of Solvency II). Advice to the Commission along these lines is also given by the Conference of Insurance Supervisory Services (see Insurance Supervisory Services, 2002).

There are other parts of the EU's structures which do not see the achievement of free trade alone as the major objective of the single market programme. Furthermore, they see uniformity of regulation as important in the creation of a single market. For example, in European Commission (2000) it says, 'Services should be available throughout the Union regardless of frontiers ... Service provision from Amsterdam to Athens should be as straightforward as from Amsterdam to Rotterdam.' As that document makes clear, to create a single market on such a basis would require more similar regulatory frameworks in a whole range of areas, including product regulation.[5] Part of the proposed action plan of that document involves greater harmonisation.

Given this conflict between progress within the insurance field itself and a wider agenda on the part of the Commission as a whole, it is worth returning to the debate about the desirability of mutual recognition, as compared with harmonisation. So far we have established that mutual recognition is sufficient to facilitate free trade but not that it is preferable.

---

5   Indeed, arguably it would require harmonisation of legal systems, tax systems, pensions systems, social security systems and language throughout the EU: see below.

Harmonisation versus mutual recognition

Those who believe in harmonisation of regulation argue that the lack of freedom of establishment in practice vindicates their view that harmonisation of regulation is necessary for the full development of free trade. It is argued that mutual recognition is confusing for consumers and that the frictional cost of multiple regulatory systems impedes trade and competition. This is the thrust of European Commission (2000). However, this is far from clear. There are many impediments to trade in financial services. Even if harmonisation of financial regulation takes place there would seem to be cultural and legal barriers that make it harder for an individual from one EU country to purchase products from another. In time, these impediments, which arise from differences in tax systems, language barriers, differences in basic legal codes, differences in social insurance systems and differences in the development of securities markets, may break down. However, it is not clear that the absence of regulatory harmonisation itself is a great impediment to trade. That case needs to be proven, and the author is not aware of any rigorous evidence put forward in favour of that proposition.

Potentially there are severe negative effects of harmonisation of regulation. Harmonisation can prevent the process of market discovery whereby the best approaches to regulation can be discovered and copied. From a public choice perspective, it centralises regulatory power and can make regulators more distant from political accountability and from the operation of the market, thus leading to over-regulation. There may be fewer restraints on regulation to prevent it becoming overbearing because market participants are less likely to be put at a 'competitive disadvantage' by the action of regulation if regulation is uniform across a number of countries. There is no incentive to update regulation so centralisation can fossilise out-of-date practices.

It is also important to note that in order to change regulation multilateral agreement is necessary between parties that may have fundamentally different views. Again, this can lead to regulation becoming fossilised. Solvency II will probably not be implemented until 2007, and discussion has been ongoing for some time. If regulation becomes fossilised, sometimes companies' own risk management practices can become tied into regulatory practices and themselves become out of date. Finally, it is very difficult to ensure that regulation determined at the international level is appropriate for a range of different countries that may have different cultures, different legal systems, different traditions, different languages, different self-regulatory structures and different market infrastructure. The cost of unifying regulation in such circumstances may be huge. Indeed, the task may be impossible if the regulations are administered under different forms of legal code. As has been noted above, harmonisation of regulation might take place at great cost, and it then might be found that greater trade in services does not develop because of these other factors. Adam Ridley's paper in this volume covers this issue in greater detail. However, it is worth noting some points specifically in relation to the insurance example.

EU Insurance Supervisory Services (2002) suggests that regulators in different EU countries have quite different objectives: 'Regulatory styles within the Community differ, varying from regimes with a "zero failure" target to "market-based" regimes where orderly exits of failed companies are allowed and even expected' (para. 2.1.2).

Even where that document tries to define common principles

to which all regulators in all countries adhere, it is unconvincing. The common principles are 'safeguarding the solvency of all firms' and 'protection of customers' rights' (para. 2.5.5). Both these statements are so general as to be meaningless, as are statements such as 'ensuring consumer protection' used by Creedon (2002) to describe the objectives of harmonised regulation. Is the consumer to be protected from insurer failure or simply from entering into a contract that is different from the one he was led to believe he was entering into? Depending on the answer to that question, one could develop completely different regulatory regimes. These differences in philosophy indicate the difficulty of harmonising regulation when there are no agreed principles upon which regulation is based.

It could also be argued that the system of mutual recognition is potentially beneficial. There is no reason to suppose that we are able to discover the optimal regulatory system easily. Indeed, if one looks at the relatively low-level harmonised aspects of the EU life insurance solvency requirements, they are based on techniques developed in the 1880s and are well behind 'state of the art'. But obtaining agreement on meaningful change amongst all EU countries is extremely difficult (see also the comment above about the likely date of the conclusion of the Solvency II process). The process of mutual recognition, whereby countries do not try to harmonise regulatory systems, can help the discovery process. Consumers can choose between products regulated under different systems.[6] Regulators can learn from each other. Voters can compare the costs of different regulatory systems.

---

6   The author would argue that competition between systems of regulation that evolve in a market is better than competition between regulatory systems of different states. Nevertheless, competition between regulatory systems of different states, it is being argued here, is better than a single regulator across all states.

In fact, it is pertinent to ask why we should try to harmonise regulatory systems across fifteen (to become 25) EU countries with very different traditions, legal systems, tax systems and structures within their savings markets. One could allow, as part of the process of regulatory competition within the single market area, bilateral or multilateral agreements between countries that could decide for themselves whether the costs of harmonisation outweigh the benefits. Those countries that had the most similar structures and had the most to gain from trade may be more likely to harmonise (for example, the UK, Ireland and Holland). This would seem to be a more vital and vibrant approach to the process of increasing trade transparency. Indeed, it is likely that, given the freedom to do so, countries within the single market would adopt aspects of the regulatory regimes used in other countries with more similar cultures and legal systems.[7]

Conclusion

Harmonisation of financial regulation is not necessary for free trade. The development of the single market does not require such harmonisation, although not all EU countries would interpret the phrase 'single market' in the same way. Harmonisation of regulation may involve fewer frictional costs under a single regulatory system. But there are, in turn, great costs of harmonisation. These costs include overt costs but also the costs of not being able to use the discovery processes of regulatory

---

7   For example, if it were possible, the UK could adopt some of the principles underlying Canadian and US insurance supervision that are based on more modern techniques of risk management than the EU system of prudential reserving requirements.

competition. Furthermore, harmonisation could be achieved only to find that there were other frictional impediments to trade. Harmonisation of regulation is unlikely to be beneficial within a free trade area, yet harmonisation is not necessary for free trade to exist. The approach of mutual recognition, as used in the area of insurance in the EU, is more appropriate than harmonisation. However, even here it could be argued that the small amount of regulation that has been harmonised is, in fact, too great. In this particular instance, this is not because the regulations themselves lead to onerous solvency requirements on companies. Rather, the harmonised regulations institution-alise accounting, reserving and risk management practices that are out of date. A move to complete mutual recognition and the removal of any harmonised regulations would enable countries that wished to do so to harmonise aspects of their regulations on the basis of bilateral or multilateral negotiations, if it was believed that this would reduce the frictional costs of trade between those countries. It would also enable EU countries to cooperate in a similar way with non-EU countries. Finally, such an approach would allow countries that wished to do so to use regulatory mechanisms that were allowed to evolve freely within the market. Because of freedom of establishment, there would be direct competition between such free markets and more regulated markets: consumers would be able to exercise a choice between regulatory regimes when purchasing products.

References

Bollick, C. (1994), *European Federalism: Lessons from America*, IEA Occasional Paper 93, IEA, London.

Booth, P. M. (2003), 'Who should regulate financial markets?',
    Economic Affairs, vol. 23, no. 3.

Creedon, S. (2002), 'Solvency II – EU Regulation', paper
    presented to the Faculty and Institute of Actuaries' Life
    Convention.

Daly, M. (2003), 'Ireland: a Centre for EU Life', *The Actuary*, Jan./
    Feb., Stable Inn Actuarial Society.

European Commission (2000), 'An Internal Market Strategy for
    Financial Services', COM(2000)888 of 29.12.2000, European
    Communities.

Hairs, C. J., Belsham, D. J., Bryson, N. M., George, C. M.,
    Hare, D. J. P., Smith, D. A. and Thompson, S. (2002), 'Fair
    valuation of liabilities', *British Actuarial Journal*, vol. 8, part 2:
    203–340.

Insurance Supervisory Services (2002), 'Prudential Supervision
    of Insurance Undertakings', Report of the Conference of
    Insurance Supervisory Services of the Member States of the
    European Union.

Kirzner, I. M. (1992), *The Meaning of the Market Process*,
    Routledge, London.

8 PRIORITIES FOR INTERNATIONAL FINANCIAL REGULATION

Adam Ridley[1]

Introduction

When I was an economist in the Treasury, I spent a fascinating eighteen months studying the impact on the British economy of joining the 'Common Market', as what is now known as the European Union was then commonly called. My colleagues and I tried to measure the effect of liberalisation, from eliminating tariffs and non-tariff barriers to permit 'free trade' in goods – not in agriculture or services. We concluded that the *static* benefits of liberalisation (arising from shifts *along* existing supply and demand curves) would be significant, although offset in part by the costs of EU membership such as the Common Agricultural Policy. That evaluation was reflected in the government's historic 1971 White Paper, in which EU membership was commended to the nation. I also concluded that in time there would be substantial dynamic benefits as well, as 'long-run' supply and demand curves shifted in response to the enlarged market and greater competition in the trading sectors.

By the mid-1980s tariffs had been removed, non-tariff barriers were under pressure in goods trade and the movement to sup-

---

1   This paper contains the personal views of the author, and does not represent the policies of the London Investment Banking Association (LIBA) of which the author is Director General.

press competitive distortions arising from public ownership and industrial subsidy was gathering speed. However, there had still been little or no progress on the services front. I suspected that there were big potential gains from free trade in services, as well as goods, so I was delighted when Lord Cockfield launched the European Commission programme 'Completing the Internal Market' in 1985 to liberalise trade in the Community's services sector. It is notable how little progress has been made since then. For the London Investment Banking Association (LIBA) and its members (largely investment banks and securities houses operating internationally) the creation of a well-run, liberalised international marketplace through the Financial Services Action Plan (FSAP) and other related reforms appeared vital. Merely cutting margins in securities dealing to competitive levels would bring big benefits for savers and companies alike. But the FSAP is scarcely 'moving forward' at all, despite the universal pious protestations about its importance.

In the early 21st century the Treasury and the Financial Services Authority (FSA) were consulting on the creation of a single regulatory system, on the Financial Services and Markets Bill (FSMB) and Act (FSMA), the 100-odd statutory instruments giving effect to it, and the thousands of pages of FSA policy papers, discussion papers, consultation papers and draft Rules. The FSA was committed from the start to a very thorough process of open consultation with market participants, experts, professionals and interested parties generally. This unprecedented experience has demonstrated that such consultation processes are essential to success in an ambitious regulatory reform, *even inside a single country.*

Just as the FSMB was nearing the end of its parliamentary passage in mid-2000, the French EU presidency triggered another important train of events – which is still far from over. The EU set up the Group of Wise Men under Alexandre Lamfalussy to advise on ways of reviving the FSAP (see the chapter by Lamfalussy in this volume).

As the debate about the problems with the FSAP evolved, the following issue became evident. Debates about the implementation of FSAP always turned to a consideration of institutions or process. The policy issues always seemed secondary in practice. As the Wise Men suggested, FSAP was stuck because the issues were being dealt with at the wrong political or institutional level; in the wrong way; with too little consultation; and so on. Does this matter? The EU is a gigantic dynamic experiment in international institutional and process design. When something goes wrong, process is very likely to be a major cause. What is so special about finding that this is true of financial sector integration?

In fact, there is something special about financial services; and there is something systematic about what has been going wrong. Some of the reasons are obvious, some not. In this chapter, I will explain why *process* is so important; then sketch some of the consequences; and then focus on some conclusions about how to put matters right.

What is so special about international financial sector integration?

The provision of financial services and the conduct of financial markets have attracted government attention and actions, whether by law, regulation, formal supervision or informal oversight; by encouragement of self-regulation; or by both governmental and self-regulation. So programmes for integrating the financial sectors of fifteen very heterogeneous economies and societies are bound to throw up many 'differences' (to use a neutral word) which will need somehow to be reconciled. Some of the most important *objective* factors are as follows:

History is a powerful influence on national attitudes: In countries that have experienced systemic disasters such as hyperinflation or major scandals of consumer exploitation, many people may still distrust their own national government. They may trust only an integrated EU market with a very powerful and competent central authority. At the other end of the scale, others may trust their own government and no other to maintain the domestic consumer protection for which they have had to fight for decades. Then there are those who know little of what other governments do as financial regulators, and who may well suspect them of one-sided and nationalistic motives and devious behaviour. Ignorance and prejudice can be a potent mixture, even in small quantities.

Legal systems differ greatly: There are fundamental differences between common law and civil code countries; and between those with or without written constitutions. At a more modest but still very important level, many countries do not have anything resembling trusts or trustees. Some do not recognise the legal concept (so beloved of regulators) of a safe harbour. And concepts of fiduciary duty probably differ radically.

Constitutions and institutions differ: Some states are federal, others unitary; some have more integrated domestic regulators, others have separate regulators for banking and insurance; some have extensive and others limited dependence on self-regulation.

Attitudes differ: Some countries believe in delegating regulation to a nominated authority like the UK's FSA. Others believe (and are so organised) that their delegated regulation should always be subject to the scrutiny of the legislature, neither trusting the technicians to be independent nor, perhaps, accepting that 'technical details' can be decided properly in what they believe is a political vacuum.

Financial market variability

Important though all these considerations are, they are only part of the problem. When economists, officials, market participants, financiers, regulators, litigators or industry representatives are drawn into the practical detail of how financial markets work, they learn quickly that they are very complex and differ very greatly in many senses. Markets can be structured in different ways in different countries; and risks and procedures that are essentially the same in different sectors can be handled or undertaken in very different ways in the same country.

Such variability is generally much greater and much more significant than are differences in methods of production and distribution of conventional manufactured and industrial goods. I will describe this phenomenon as 'financial market variability'. The factors underlying the phenomenon are not unique to the financial sectors. While they are only of secondary importance in most goods markets, they are central to the nature of most financial sector activity.

Ronald Coase: the theoretical basis of financial market variability

Why should there be so much intrinsic variablity? We can help to answer this using the ideas of a legal and economic debate, which derives from a very profound article by the Nobel Prize-winning economist Ronald Coase (1961). It introduces the problem of the 'wandering cattle and the wheat growers'.

Nomadic cattle herders come to an unfenced agricultural area devoted exclusively to wheat growing. They are only too happy when their cattle find excellent food in the wheat fields. But the farmers are not. If the herders have no, or only partial, responsibility for the damage they do, cattle production will thrive, but grain production will suffer badly and the community will be worse off. However, if the cattle herders are required by law or regulation to bear the full cost of the fencing and of the damage their cattle cause, then private and social costs and benefits will be equal, and society will be at a welfare optimum.

Consider the mirror-image case. In an area, say a 'common' hitherto devoted to nomadic cattle herding, wheat farmers arrive who wish to keep the cattle out of their fields by erecting fences. This is to the detriment of the herders. If any wheat grower can fence off any land he chooses, albeit at his own cost, wheat production will thrive, but cattle farming will shrink dramatically and the community will be worse off. *However*, if the wheat growers are required by law or regulation to bear the full costs of the loss to the cattle farmers as well as the cost of fencing, then private and social cost will be equal, and society will again be at a welfare optimum.

We can go farther. The optimum balance between cattle and wheat will be the same (for given land and cattle) in *both* cases. *Coase showed that the manner in which the law and regulators assign liability will not affect the ultimate allocation of production, provided costs and benefits are properly reflected in the legal and regulatory structure.*

We can go farther still with this example. There are at least two other ways of achieving the same optimum using insurance. First, the wheat growers could be required to insure ('all risks') against damage by wandering cattle; and the underwriters specify that they must build the fences and negotiate compensation agreements with the graziers for loss of income. Alternatively, the graziers may be permitted to graze only if they take out third party insurance for damage caused by their cattle; and this time the underwriters insist it is the graziers, not the wheat growers, who should build and maintain the fences.

Fifth, but not least, one might imagine a *centralised regulatory authority* that owns and fences the area, subject to a duty to allocate land use 'fairly', meaning in such a way as to optimise the land usage. Even if the authority levies no charges on wheat growers or cattle raisers, it could perhaps in principle model social costs and benefits accurately enough to allocate the land use and fencing appropriately.

In sum, even in market interactions between such eminently physical products and factors of production as cattle, grain, fences and land, there are five (and probably more) different ways of ensuring the correct, identical, allocation of resources. Many of those ways are, or could be, incompatible.

What happens when we leave behind the world of physical objects and turn to 'pure' financial service transactions and contracts? In such transactions money passes in one direction, in exchange for some right, thus creating a financial asset – typically consisting, for example, of an obligation to pay, repay or share in profits; or contingent rights in the form of options, general or life insurance, sickness pay, pensions, and so on. The provision and distribution of the 'product' are no longer circumscribed by a physical process of production, or by the physical characteristics of the product. So for pure services, therefore, one would predict a greater variety of practice in production, distribution and regulation. The direct consequence will therefore be even more scope for discrepancies when two national marketplaces are brought together. Equally important, one would expect that the precise characteristics of such specific market niches would often be so recherché that they would be barely understood, even within a country, let alone elsewhere.

The additional influences of systemic risk, consumer protection and unfair competition

On top of this extreme underlying heterogeneity there will often be considerations of controlling systemic risk, protecting consumers and mitigating imbalances in market power and information. These will draw the authorities into an all too complex web of legal, regulatory, self-regulatory and commercial interventions. The scope for variation will be immense in these respects too, being a function of all the sorts of obvious influence cited above. Typically, from the moment these procedures were first set up, they have been rich in national idiosyncrasies. At the time they were set up, financial services were usually for home markets only. So few governments knew or cared much about what other countries did, let alone wanted to imitate them.

So when we try to bring together separate economies in a single financial marketplace, it is scarcely surprising that the process is so hard and so different from, say, unifying the market in cars.[2] When we come to the financial sectors, such as the securities markets, we are in the heart of this different world.

Sporting parallels

It is pertinent to draw an analogy to show how serious this challenge can be. Imagine that it is desired to 'integrate' (or rather reintegrate) rugby union and American football, which broke away from rugby rules in the late nineteenth century. There would be a problem. In rugby, you may pass the ball only backwards. In American football, you may pass it forwards. So integration looks impossible.

Suppose instead we are set the more modest objective of 'enlarging the single market in rugby', and that it is proposed to unite rugby league and rugby union. The differences are undoubtedly fewer, and less radical. But just what they are, which ones really matter, and what would be involved in reconciling them, is unclear to nearly all of us. Almost certainly they will be way beyond the knowledge of ministers and Treasury officials. (And who can tell whether the supporters would be interested in the resulting hybrid?) There is little chance the government could determine authoritatively whether integration was desirable or even whether it was feasible.

The process of creating an integrated financial marketplace in Europe is not unlike these rather fanciful programmes of sporting

2   In that case there were questions of safety standards, annual inspection, and so on. These constituted serious non-tariff barriers in the EU and, once solved, they revealed a further array of obstacles in the form of complex (and questionable) agreements between manufacturers, main distributors and dealers about the distribution and servicing process. However, much of this could be dealt with by classic deregulation and liberalisation.

harmonisation. If there are so many diverse ways to regulate financial markets, then one would predict that integrating them would usually be very hard work, and sometimes impossible, since the integrator will find so many differences to reconcile. It is therefore not at all surprising that the 1985 Cockfield programme has delivered less than expected; that the First Investment Services Directive (ISD1) of 1993 was flawed in some key respects and brought limited results; or that of the 42 FSAP measures, many of the most fundamental are still proving to be so problematic.

Misjudged attempts to integrate markets

If there is something special about financial services, what, then, should one do to promote EU or international financial market integration, regulation and liberalisation effectively? Whatever else, one should not maintain the recent approach of EU member governments. At the risk of parody and unfairness, it could be said that when the EU's governments and institutions put together a portfolio of measures under a label such as the FSAP, it is rather like designing a menu of dishes from a recipe book with those very flowery descriptions favoured by some of today's fashionable chefs: the ministers and senior officials involved choose between items such as a light dish of collateral served on a bed of mature master product agreements; followed as entrée by a single passport for all markets, with a sauce of fortified national stock exchanges of at least four kinds; followed by a pension *bombe* Alaska as dessert; all washed down with a … Yet almost no one has any idea what these fine-sounding and seductive titles mean, let alone whether they are attainable, beneficial or can be put into effect on a sensible timescale.

Systematic errors and pathological outcomes

When policy-makers commit themselves in such a way to integrating and regulating parts of the market in which common policies are in truth hard or impossible to achieve – and typically to vast programmes with rigid and very short deadlines – then there are a number of standard problems that will regularly arise. These problems are described below.

1 Technicians and negotiators will not be able to reach agreement: perhaps the least bad outcome in some cases. Thus in the case of ISD1, there was no agreement about how to harmonise Conduct of Business Rules. So the politicians left the responsibility with host states.

2 The technicians and regulators may agree a common policy but the regulatory solution may be deemed politically unacceptable, so another solution is imposed through the 'political' rather than the technical part of the consultative process. This could be imposed by the European Commission, as in the final decisions on the ISD1 proposed in November 2002; by the Council of Ministers, or by the Parliament (e.g. in the case of the Take-over Directive). This is not a guaranteed recipe for disaster, but it is a reliable route to very indifferent policies and very poor results.

3 The technicians and negotiators can agree, just, but in so doing have to overcome the deep distrust felt by many members vis-à-vis other members; whether for the quality of law enforcement and regulation, the morals of public servants, politicians and legislators, or the effectiveness of the European Commission in ensuring that directives are implemented consistently and effectively. So to reduce the scope for such deviant behaviour

to the minimum, the directive text is exceptionally specific, lengthy and, perhaps worst of all, rigid and prescriptive (e.g. the Prospectus Directive implementation proposals that have been in the process of being developed since late 2002).

4 Technicians and negotiators reach a 'politically correct' consensus, defined as giving everyone a part of what they asked for. But the outcome may make little operational sense (e.g. the case of ISD2).

5 A fifth possibility arises when technicians and negotiators, recognising that little movement is possible, agree to construct what is termed a common policy; but in reality it is little more than a patchwork of members' existing national practices, stitched together with the thread of communautaire rhetoric. This can be sensible, of course, if the issue calls for subsidiarity or mutual recognition rather than harmonisation anyway. But it may immobilise policy development at EU level for many years.

6 Then there is a sixth case, when a member fears exploitation, for example, of its consumers by businesses in other member states. It sees in an EU initiative an opportunity to protect its own producers and markets or, better still, to reverse the effect of competition and to 'repatriate' once-domestic business that has gone elsewhere. In such circumstances the rhetoric of market integration, a level playing field, etc., provides an excellent camouflage for the re-erection of barriers to competition and mercantilism of many kinds (e.g. the Prospectus Directive).

Outcomes such as these have been seen in many major FSAP measures. The elaboration of Community institutions in recent years has made it harder to handle FSAP measures. It has created more opportunity for political interference through co-decision; more scope for discriminating against minorities through qualified majority voting; and could tempt members of the Committee of European Services Regulators (CESR) to reverse the political decisions embodied in a directive, for protectionist and nationalistic motives. Such problems will obviously be more serious and will affect more of the proposals under review if ministers decide to introduce new regulatory policies very rapidly. Matters are made particularly difficult if the deadlines for completion are inflexible and arbitrary as well as very short.

How can we avoid such problems? Process is fundamental. Ensuring the right process will not conjure agreement out of contradiction. But it will help us to find common ground if it is to be found; or warn us off when there is no consensus to be had.

How should we integrate financial markets and regulations?

The most important answer to this question is 'Look before you leap'. What might it mean in this context? There are five important characteristics of a more effective process.

Clarify objectives and constraints

Political leaders and advisers should look beyond the sound-bite programme labels such as the 'single market' or 'financial services action plan'. It is essential to define the specific, concrete goal to be achieved and, as far as possible, the practical means by which those goals can be achieved. In that light, are each nation's political, institutional and legal regimes compatible or contradictory?

Is the goal only worth pursuing if everyone goes all the way? Or would the goal still be worth pursuing if some dropped out? This question is a familiar one in EU policy debates under the rubric of 'variable geometry': see Wallace and Ridley (1985), for example. How important is it to implement 'all' the policy or to take it 'all the way'?

Apply the appropriate tests of costs and benefits before finally deciding to proceed

Before proceeding we should attempt to answer the following questions. Will the policy finally recommended bring material benefits? Will the costs be justified? Will both costs and benefits be acceptably distributed, even if the policy proposals are acceptable? Precise answers to such questions are notoriously hard to find, but that is no excuse for not even trying to identify any of them, as is still so common.

Consider all the alternatives available for meeting the policy goal

There may be several distinct policy methods to consider. There may also be an option of deregulation and true liberalisation, which should not be ruled out. Since policies and institutions tend to become rigid, it may be that two (or more) regulatory methods or policies could be pursued together, which will inject the vital element of competition and stimulus into innovation. Particularly where such competition is not possible and a single harmonised policy is pursued, then some regular review process should be set up. If the policy looks irreversible and risky, one should consider the possibilities of experimenting with pilot projects before implementing the policy on an EU-wide basis. We should recognise the truism, unquestioningly accepted in other areas of policy-making, that introducing good policies is not a one-off act, but a process.

Quality not speed

Integrating markets is a vast, momentous exercise that has to be pursued in the right way. Because it is so complex, meeting the tight timetables that all interested parties have wanted until recently – ministers, the European Commission, consumers and business alike – is much less important in most cases than introducing measures of high quality which do the job, even if deadlines are missed.

Consultation is essential

This, again, is accepted in other fields. This subject will be pursued at greater length below.

The parallels with monetary integration

There are interesting parallels to be drawn here with the technical and economic debate about monetary union and the introduction of the euro. We have been treated to numerous studies of this family of issues and some important broad propositions emerge from them.

Optimal currency areas

First, theoreticians have long underlined that the case for two or more countries integrating their currencies depends on the characteristics of the countries involved. The candidates should constitute an 'optimal currency' area to justify their monetary union economically. In such optimal areas, certain relationships should prevail between each potential member, such as a high degree of mobility of capital and labour, high levels of reciprocal trade and reasonably consistent or convergent expectations. By the same token, countries that do not meet such conditions would do better if they retained separate currencies. An optimal currency area cannot be defined precisely by economists. Nevertheless, these conditions do give a framework for the economic analysis of whether a particular area is likely to benefit from a currency union or not.

Other optimal areas

Also, regional economists have recognised for decades that within broad geographical zones optimal areas for uniform policy or integrated regulation may differ widely depending on the product, service, function or process under examination. Thus it would be inconceivable that the optimal areas would be identical for telecom regulation, controlling the press, physical planning, conservation of fish stocks, air-traffic control, public health administration, and so on. Optimal areas will vary widely for different financial services in the same way.

Step by step

It should also be noted that the debate about European monetary union and the policy for adopting the euro were taken forward in a measured way, step by step. Indeed, it took the best part of two generations. It was generally recognised that some states would not want to join at the start, or perhaps not join at all. On the other hand, other states might join at different dates determined above all by when they satisfied conditions determined by the key policy-makers.

Integration should bring benefits

At least one country, the UK, has gone farther, and has indicated that she should not try to join unless doing so could be shown to be in the national economic interest – at present by the findings of the Chancellor of the Exchequer's 'five economic tests'. Whatever the results of the tests, and whether or not the tests are precisely the correct tests to use, the approach ensures that substantial and well-researched study of the pluses and minuses of European monetary union for the UK is undertaken before a decision is taken to join.

Differences from the FSAP

The EU proposals for regulating a single market in financial services have evolved very differently. There has been little or no serious public debate about an optimal regulatory area or areas; nor about what to do in circumstances when optimal areas are likely to be inconsistent economically, or unacceptable politically. There has been little analysis of the impact on individual members of particular measures or of the total FSAP package, whether of costs or of benefits. Of course, there have been some interesting studies of the aggregate impact on the EU *as a whole* of truly integrated financial markets. However, these are not studies of the effect of the FSAP measures as such. With few exceptions there has been no suggestion that the financial policies and regulation implemented by individual EU members would have to meet certain minimum quality standards before they would be allowed to adopt a single financial market policy or policies. There has been no public debate about whether it would be best to let individual countries 'join the FSAP' (as it were) at different times, 'when the time is ripe'; or join in some sectors only. There has not been much discussion of the scope for allowing two policy regimes to continue in competition with one another in order to see which regime markets prefer or which works best.

The decision to adopt the FSAP as a programme was taken as being self-evidently desirable, before its potential form was sketched out at the EU level, let alone its impact studied sector by sector. In the UK neither the Treasury, the City, the Chancellor of the Exchequer, Parliament, the FSA nor the economics profession has suggested publicly that any rigorous tests be applied to decide whether the FSAP as a whole or its specific ingredients are beneficial. The same appears to be true in the other fourteen EU countries. So, the members of the EU have not 'looked before leaping' into the FSAP. Therefore we should not be surprised if implementing such measures proves to be difficult, unpopular and, in some cases, impossible.

A lesson from the Hard ECU?

Interestingly, the earlier UK debate about EMU in the early 1990s also illustrated another feature: the scope for changing monetary arrangements gradually by consent and competition rather than by imposing a top-down and comprehensive replacement for the old regime overnight. The proposal to introduce the 'Hard ECU' was put forward by some as an elegant alternative to EMU (e.g. Richards (1990) and HM Treasury (1990)). The Hard ECU was to be run at all times as the 'best-behaved currency' within the Union. Provided that the goal of 'best-behaved currency' was clearly achieved, then, in commercial life at least, weaker state currencies would gradually be replaced. The underlying generic approach obviously relates very closely to the debate about the advantages of permitting competing regulatory policies or jurisdictions (see also the chapter by Booth in this volume).

Consultation standards

Consultation is essential for successful policy development and implementation. More and more institutions and governments recognise this – and not just in the financial sector. The details of how consultation should be undertaken are not the subject of this paper. However, it is worth considering briefly some models.

The UK Treasury and the FSA developed a robust procedure in the enactment and implementation of the FSMA.[3] Some of that procedure is, indeed, now embodied in the act itself. This involves informal consultation with experts perhaps leading to (non-committal) discussion papers; published policy or discussion papers with a minimum comment period of three months (the

---

3   Unfortunately, there is no single statement of the FSA's practices, obligations or voluntary commitment. The FSMA set out certain obligations to consult and undertake cost–benefit analysis. Other statements of undertakings and performance standards are distributed over a range of FSA publications.

process may be repeated if needed when the first concrete proposals are substantially revised); then concrete proposals, draft laws, rules, statutory instruments with *another* three months' minimum consultation period. And only then the definitive regulation or rule. The same kind of procedure as that used by the FSA is embodied in the CESR's recently adopted statement (CESR, 2001). With regard to the European Commission's consultation standards, their latest proposals on governance published late in 2002 follow good practice in some respects, though not all.[4] The International Council of Securities Associations, which groups together sixteen of the principal associations representing the securities industry worldwide, has just completed work on a 'Statement on Regulatory Consultation Practices',[5] which is in many respects the most thorough treatment of the issues. Although it is particularly directed at consultation by regulators, it is equally applicable to other bodies involved in developing regulatory policy, be they individual governments, supranational or international bodies. The UK government Cabinet Office has also laid down a code for all ministries and departments of the UK government[6] which has some application to detached government agencies. This code is not mandatory, but is taken very seriously.

Consultation on ideas before firm proposals

Such codes can work but, if embraced too enthusiastically, they

---

4   Their proposals, published on 11 December 2002 as COM(2002)70 4 final, can be obtained from www.europa.en.int/comm/governance/docs/comm_standards_en.pdf.

5   Available from www.icsa.bz.

6   The UK Cabinet Office's 'Code of Practice on Written Consultation' can be found at www.cabinet-office.gov.uk/servicefirst/index/consultation.htm.

can well become bureaucratic, expensive and dangerously 'politically correct'. So it is important that consideration of the details of such codes does not divert attention from the fundamental, almost banal, issue at the heart of the consultation process – that consultation must start before minds are made up. Consultation should take place first on ends and only then, when the desired ends are clear, about possible means. Consultation should take place, as far as possible, with genuinely open minds. In rare cases, there might be an uncompromisingly committed journey to a definite goal that no amount of consultation will change.

The process of true consultation, then, is fundamentally cooperative and tentative: putting forward preliminary ideas; considering responses; modifying objectives; offering reasons and inviting them from others; testing acceptability; researching costs and benefits; solving administrative complications, and so on. Quite frequently this preliminary cycle will need to be repeated, as the British FSA has done on occasions. Key proposals are best kept malleable for some time, rather than being solidified at the outset.

There will therefore be a trade-off between speed and quality. Politics and politicians often require speed and adherence to deadlines. Wise legislation often calls for the opposite. The principles above are not novel. Successive British governments have done much to 'pre-consult' – not least the UK Treasury under the chancellorship of Sir Geoffrey Howe and Nigel Lawson from 1979 to 1989. Lamfalussy's Wise Men have recommended this very specifically.

Legislating for consultation on ideas

Eloquent though the group of Wise Men was, the response to their report has been inadequate. The EU has provided for a substantial measure of guaranteed transparency and consultation once Directives are agreed, but the commitments to consult on ideas in the formative stages are very limited. Thus a key European text – the EU Governance White Paper – does not require automatic transparency and consultation in levels one and two and for comitology[7], even if it sets sensible standards for it at later stages in the legislative process.

Guaranteeing consultation on ideas at the start of all intended policy initiatives (except, of course, in emergencies) is not a sufficient condition for wise government or policy-making. However, the case for consultation being a fundamental necessary condition in international financial policy-making even more than in domestic policy-making is surely exceptionally strong. As well as favouring rational debate, consultation and transparency much reduce the scope for concealing discreditable decision-making. At this moment – when the EU is about to embark on a Treaty revision that may be the last for many years – it is time for the Convention on the Future European Constitution to commend, and for the subsequent inter-governmental conference (IGC) to adopt, a treaty amendment requiring mandatory pre-consultation except in emergencies, that is consultation on ideas and the appropriate degree of transparency. In the meantime, present EU institutions should ensure that they follow such consultation procedures.

A concluding comment

If our ultimate goal is free trade in services we should be looking for deregulation, rather than at the regulatory architecture per se. We

---

7   Comitology powers are those where the Council reserves the right to exercise directly implementing powers itself, subject to the opinion but not the right of veto of the European Parliament.

should be looking for simplification and the removal of obstacles. Markets flourish when tariff and non-tariff barriers are cut back and irrelevant political and institutional burdens are stripped away. The key to the single market, in other words, is liberalisation: removing bureaucracy. If one requires the world's regulators to reconstruct markets internationally very quickly, they will, being regulators, look for their answers in regulatory constructs. Do we really want that? Not if the goal is liberalisation. Openness and consultation and proceeding at a measured pace can help correct that balance and help restrain regulatory authorities from creating a single market that is an over-regulated market.

References

CESR (2001), 'Public Statement of Consultation Practices', Committee of European Securities Regulators Paper ref. CESR/01-007c, available from www.europefesco.org.

Coase, R. (1961), 'The problem of Social Cost', *Journal of Law and Economics* 3.

HM Treasury (1990), *The UK proposals for a European Monetary Fund and a 'hard ECU': making progress towards economic and monetary union in Europe*, Treasury Bulletin, autumn 1990, HM Treasury, London.

Richards, O. P. (1990), *The hard ECU and alternative paths to European monetary union: the case for an evolutionary Stage 2*, LSE Financial Markets Group: Special Paper no. 29, London School of Economics, London.

Wallace, H., and Ridley, A. (1985), *Europe: The Challenge of Diversity*, Chatham House Report no. 29, Royal Institute of International Affairs, Routledge & Kegan Paul, London.

9 THE GOAL OF A SINGLE EUROPEAN FINANCIAL MARKET

Tim Congdon

Introduction

The goal of a single European financial market – analogous to the single European market in industrial products that has been forged since the Treaty of Rome in 1957 – is, on the face of it, wholly worthy and desirable. Free cross-border trade in industrial products has undoubtedly brought great benefits to Europe's consumers through facilitating regional specialisation and economies of scale. Surely, free cross-border trade in financial services should bring similar gains.

The purpose of this paper is not to deny that free trade in financial services is 'a good thing', but to wonder whether the advocates of a European single market in financial products have quite understood the realities of international finance at the start of the 21st century. In particular, they appear not to have noticed that the ideal of a single European financial market has been bypassed by the fact of a single global market in wholesale financial products. Further, and somewhat ironically, the attitude of Europe's governments towards this wholesale market has been at best ambivalent and at worst hostile, raising the question of whether leading policy-makers have any clear notion of where they are going.

The historical context

In the years immediately following World War II, the world lacked integrated international capital markets of the kind that had existed in the heyday of the gold standard before 1914. Corporate fund-raising was, almost exclusively, local and specific to nations. Thus, an American company would issue bonds denominated in dollars in an American financial centre (usually New York) to American investors subject to the laws of the USA and the regulations of the New York Stock Exchange. Perhaps the most important reason for this localisation of financial business was exchange control. Because companies and investors in most of Europe and other continents could not remit funds freely across borders, companies could not consider raising funds except in their country of residence.

The USA – which did not have exchange controls – was a possible exception, but the national market was so large relative to financial markets elsewhere that it was hardly worth management time to explore alternatives in the immediate post-war years. However, in the late 1950s US companies started to leave deposits in banks outside the USA, principally in London. These dollars were called 'euro-dollars' to distinguish them from dollars in the USA, but they were fully interchangeable with dollars anywhere. Dollar-banking business in London had a huge advantage over dollar-banking business in the USA, in that it was not subject to the costly and restrictive regulations imposed on banks after the Great Depression. Over the 25 years to 1982, euro-dollar banking boomed in London and some other centres, growing much more rapidly than domestic banking in the USA.

But this was only the beginning of the internationalisation of financial activity. International business can be conducted in any convertible currency by the banks of any nation. For most of the 1960s and 1970s the euro-currency markets involved only the three leading convertible currencies of the time, the dollar, the Deutschmark and the Swiss franc, but the abolition of exchange controls by the UK in 1979 was followed by similar liberalisations across the industrial world. By the 1990s international banking business, now in a wide assortment of currencies, was larger than any domestic banking system except those of the USA and Japan.

But it is not just banking which can be internationalised. The businesses of bond issuance, underwriting and trading can also be carried out anywhere. Assuming exchange freedom, funds can be remitted to any nation (or any group of nations) once they have been raised. Moreover, the raising of the funds does not have to be constrained by borders. The issuers and underwriters have of course to operate subject to the laws of a particular jurisdiction and out of a building in a particular locality, but they can choose the jurisdiction and locality most suitable for the purpose, and then seek funds from any country.

By the 1990s the wholesale dimension of both banking and bond market activity had been largely internationalised. National markets (still subject to national laws and regulations) competed with the international (or 'euro') markets, but generally they lost ground. The international market could handle larger deals and, with its relative freedom from government regulation, it was characterised by narrower spreads and greater liquidity. Bond issuance in the 'international' markets is now broadly the same as in all the national markets of the world combined. Figures 1 and 2, based on data compiled by the Bank for International Settlements, show how international issuance has risen relative to the combined national total and seems to be about to overtake it. (The outstanding

Figure 1 **Net issues of bonds and notes**
Quarterly data from BIS, $bn

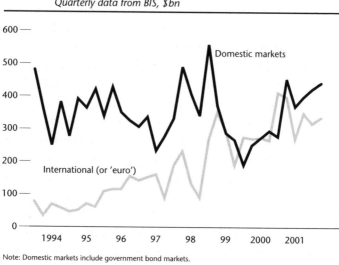

Note: Domestic markets include government bond markets.

stock of national bonds – which includes bonds issued to finance government debts – is still much larger.)

The paradox of policy at the European level

The narrow view of European regulators

Policy-makers in some countries had only a dim awareness of the scale of the revolution that was under way. Part of the trouble may have been terminological. As the new single European currency introduced in 1999 was called the euro, the old label ('euro-dollar' and affiliates) had become inconvenient. Despite the massive scale of non-national financial business, a universally accepted name for

Figure 2 **Bonds and notes, outstanding stock**
Quarterly data from BIS, $bn

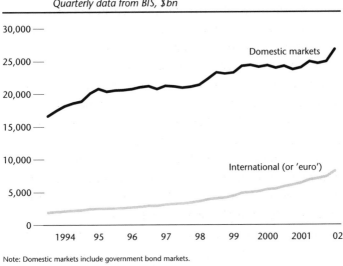

Note: Domestic markets include government bond markets.

it has yet to emerge. If people do not know what something is to be called, there should be no surprise that they do not talk about it very much.

In the rest of this paper the non-national markets will be called 'the offshore markets', but others might prefer the terms 'non-national' or 'international'. The trouble with replacing the term 'euro' by 'international' – which seems to be the emerging practice – is that it overlooks agents' ability to raise money in regulated national markets that are foreign to them. For example, a European company might borrow in the USA subject to American laws and regulations (creating 'yankee' securities, as they are called) or in Japan subject to Japanese laws and regulations (creating 'samurai' securities). Yankee and samurai securities are surely international in character, but they are not 'euro' in the old pre-single-currency sense. 'Offshore' seems better, but this is a matter of taste.

It is essential to realise that by the end of the twentieth century European governments and companies – just like the US, or indeed Japanese, government and companies – were able to take advantage of the offshore markets. As an early by-product of European currency unification, their nations had all abolished exchange controls. So by the end of the 1990s, assuming a reasonable credit rating, there was no technical difficulty about a Spanish or Italian company issuing dollar or Swiss franc bonds, with the deal arranged and underwritten by a US investment bank in London, and with the purchasers of the bond being all over the world, including – for example – Japan and the Middle East. The dollars might be converted back ('swapped') into pesetas or lira, or by 1999 into euros, but even the currency exposure could be covered by the appropriate forward transaction.

European tax authorities see the wider view!

Thus, at the start of the 21st century, the notion of 'a single European financial market' has become parochial and old-fashioned. The earnest and well-meaning European civil servants and economists pressing for such a market need to wake up to the world in which they are living. As it happens, tax authorities across Europe are very much awake to one aspect of the international bond market. Most bonds in the international markets are issued in bearer form, with beneficial ownership established by physical possession of the bond certificate. This characteristic of the bonds has vital fiscal consequences.

Because the bonds are not registered, the tax authorities cannot trace their owners. As is notorious, holders of the bonds cut the coupons off the bonds, take them to a paying agent (typically in Luxembourg or Switzerland) and do not disclose the income to their tax inspectors. As the offshore bond market has boomed, so the tax receipts and fiscal solvency of European governments have been undermined by increasing tax evasion. Europe's governments have responded by demanding that all bond issuers in a European location (including London) should pay a withholding tax. This would not destroy the offshore bond market, but it would cause the market to move out of a European centre. The underwriting and arranging activity would leave London, and the coupon-paying activity would leave Luxembourg.

The British government has resisted the imposition of withholding taxes, not least because offshore financial activity has become a big business in its own right, creating many highly paid jobs in London. (It is plausible that offshore financial activity generates over 1.5 per cent and possibly over 2 per cent of the UK's gross domestic product, but the exact figure is not known. There are problems distinguishing offshore financial activity from other types of financial business.) At any rate, the spectacle of government and regulatory intervention in current market structures is more than a little odd. Europe's governments are simultaneously engaged in trying to promote 'a single European financial market' and to expel from Europe an already established single global financial market in wholesale products. Ironically, the established market is not only one from which European companies benefit, but one that adds to European incomes and employment. Indeed, some European governments have even been known to issue bonds in the offshore markets which in other contexts they denounce!

European policy-making and economic reality

Tension between professed theoretical ideals and grubby market reality is not new in European history. However, a first step towards wisdom in public policy must be for the European Commission to recognise that over-regulation and over-taxation would amount to the exile of the offshore markets from the EU. European companies, financial institutions and even governments (yes, even governments) would continue to borrow from the offshore markets, but these markets would be located elsewhere, probably in Switzerland, but perhaps in more remote places like New York, Hong Kong or Dubai. To say this is not to condone tax evasion, but just as the collection of taxes is a national prerogative so the prevention of tax evasion is a national problem.

The relevance of the single European financial market

But if there is already a vast global market in banking and bond finance, is there still any point in 'a single European financial market'? The answer is that Europe's potential gains from international financial integration have indeed already been largely reaped by the boom in the offshore markets in the last 40 years. However, there are at least two respects in which a case for European financial integration might still have considerable relevance.

The first arises because the offshore revolution has been a revolution of the wholesale markets. The members of the EU – like all countries with convertible currencies – may have a single wholesale market in banking and bond products, but do not have a single retail market in financial products. The precise boundary between wholesale and retail markets is a matter for discussion. Obviously, the scale of the representative transactions is much greater in the wholesale markets than in the retail. But a perhaps more fundamental difference between the retail and wholesale markets is that the participants in the latter are virtually all corporate and are therefore not covered by codes of consumer protection intended to help the small saver. Such codes – like the supporting legislation – are virtually always national in their provenance and applicability.

The legislation, taxation and regulation of retail savings are therefore national, and the marketing and administration of retail products, as well as the management of retail funds, are also national. Almost certainly, useful gains from economies of scale in marketing and administration would become possible if such 'national barriers' to European financial integration could be removed. Some research does indicate that the costs to the consumer of the marketing and administration of US mutual funds are lower than similar costs on equivalent products in the member states of the EU. But the cost differential is tiny, a matter of a few basis points. It is worth asking whether European nations are prepared for the institutional upheaval required to establish a large-scale, American-style market in retail savings products.

A key driver in all retail savings products is their tax treatment. By implication, members of the EU would need to agree on a uniform tax status for new forms of retail savings product, if such products were to be sold throughout the EU. But that would necessitate extensive collaboration between tax authorities of a kind that is now difficult to imagine, as well as acceptance of the budgetary implications. Without far greater political integration, including possibly the creation of a European-wide tax-collecting agency, the goal of a single European market in retail financial products will struggle to make progress.

The second gap left by the development of the offshore market is in the area of equity finance. The offshore markets are predominantly in banking and bond products. Although they have extended to convertibles and an extraordinary assortment of exotic and hybrid securities, the issuance of equities – like that of retail savings products – remains very much on a national basis. Of course, new issues of equities for large companies may be marketed in several countries and may be underwritten by banks from all round the world, but the destination of the funds is a company with a definite national location.

Companies are located in a particular country which – in the final analysis – has the job of enforcing the ownership rights inherent in the equity securities. Shareholders need the confidence provided by a clearly defined national status to be sure that the specified nation's laws will protect their property rights. The offshore markets deal in euro-currency loans, euro-bonds and euro-convertibles. But the concept of 'euro-equities' is not meaningful. (Some lawyers have tried to devise a euro-equity category, and failed.) Equities are ultimately national financial products, because the companies that issue them must have a legally defined national status.

It follows that a fully fledged 'single European equity market' could not emerge unless there were a single European state with a single set of laws. Companies will remain national as long as there are separate nations with their own laws. This does not mean that such matters as settlement procedures and the rules governing takeovers cannot be made more 'European'. Here, perhaps, is the area where the goal of increased European financial integration has most substance.

But the benefits of such integration should not be exaggerated.

The last twenty years have already seen an explosion in cross-border equity activity, both within Europe and between Europe and the rest of the world, and it is difficult to believe that the wider benefits to economic efficiency from a single European equity trading platform would be all that dramatic. Moreover, there is the obvious point that if agreement on settlement procedures, takeover rules and so on is beneficial at the European level, it must also be beneficial, to an ever greater degree, at the global level. Once that is accepted, there is nothing particularly special about the European dimension of international financial integration.

ABOUT THE IEA

The Institute is a research and educational charity (No. CC 235 351), limited by guarantee. Its mission is to improve understanding of the fundamental institutions of a free society with particular reference to the role of markets in solving economic and social problems.

The IEA achieves its mission by:

- a high-quality publishing programme
- conferences, seminars, lectures and other events
- outreach to school and college students
- brokering media introductions and appearances

The IEA, which was established in 1955 by the late Sir Antony Fisher, is an educational charity, not a political organisation. It is independent of any political party or group and does not carry on activities intended to affect support for any political party or candidate in any election or referendum, or at any other time. It is financed by sales of publications, conference fees and voluntary donations.

In addition to its main series of publications the IEA also publishes a quarterly journal, *Economic Affairs*, and has two specialist programmes – Environment and Technology, and Education.

The IEA is aided in its work by a distinguished international Academic Advisory Council and an eminent panel of Honorary Fellows. Together with other academics, they review prospective IEA publications, their comments being passed on anonymously to authors. All IEA papers are therefore subject to the same rigorous independent refereeing process as used by leading academic journals.

IEA publications enjoy widespread classroom use and course adoptions in schools and universities. They are also sold throughout the world and often translated/reprinted.

Since 1974 the IEA has helped to create a world-wide network of 100 similar institutions in over 70 countries. They are all independent but share the IEA's mission.

Views expressed in the IEA's publications are those of the authors, not those of the Institute (which has no corporate view), its Managing Trustees, Academic Advisory Council members or senior staff.

Members of the Institute's Academic Advisory Council, Honorary Fellows, Trustees and Staff are listed on the following page.

The Institute gratefully acknowledges financial support for its publications programme and other work from a generous benefaction by the late Alec and Beryl Warren.

173

Other papers recently published by the IEA include:

WHO, What and Why?

Transnational Government, Legitimacy and the World Health Organization
Roger Scruton
Occasional Paper 113; ISBN 0 255 36487 3
£8.00

The World Turned Rightside Up

A New Trading Agenda for the Age of Globalisation
John C. Hulsman
Occasional Paper 114; ISBN 0 255 36495 4
£8.00

The Representation of Business in English Literature

Introduced and edited by Arthur Pollard
Readings 53; ISBN 0 255 36491 1
£12.00

Anti-Liberalism 2000

The Rise of New Millennium Collectivism
David Henderson
Occasional Paper 115; ISBN 0 255 36497 0
£7.50

Capitalism, Morality and Markets

Brian Griffiths, Robert A. Sirico, Norman Barry & Frank Field

Readings 54; ISBN 0 255 36496 2

£7.50

A Conversation with Harris and Seldon

Ralph Harris & Arthur Seldon

Occasional Paper 116; ISBN 0 255 36498 9

£7.50

Malaria and the DDT Story

Richard Tren & Roger Bate

Occasional Paper 117; ISBN 0 255 36499 7

£10.00

A Plea to Economists Who Favour Liberty: Assist the Everyman

Daniel B. Klein

Occasional Paper 118; ISBN 0 255 36501 2

£10.00

Waging the War of Ideas

John Blundell

Occasional Paper 119; ISBN 0 255 36500 4

£10.00

The Changing Fortunes of Economic Liberalism

Yesterday, Today and Tomorrow
David Henderson
Occasional Paper 105 (new edition); ISBN 0 255 36520 9
£12.50

The Global Education Industry

Lessons from Private Education in Developing Countries
James Tooley
Hobart Paper 141 (new edition); ISBN 0 255 36503 9
£12.50

Saving Our Streams

*The Role of the Anglers' Conservation Association in
Protecting English and Welsh Rivers*
Roger Bate
Research Monograph 53; ISBN 0 255 36494 6
£10.00

Better Off Out?

The Benefits or Costs of EU Membership
Brian Hindley & Martin Howe
Occasional Paper 99 (new edition); ISBN 0 255 36502 0
£10.00

Buckingham at 25

Freeing the Universities from State Control
Edited by James Tooley
Readings 55; ISBN 0 255 36512 8
£15.00

Lectures on Regulatory and Competition Policy

Irwin M. Stelzer
Occasional Paper 120; ISBN 0 255 36511 X
£12.50

Misguided Virtue

False Notions of Corporate Social Responsibility
David Henderson
Hobart Paper 142; ISBN 0 255 36510 1
£12.50

HIV and Aids in Schools

The Political Economy of Pressure Groups and Miseducation
Barrie Craven, Pauline Dixon, Gordon Stewart & James Tooley
Occasional Paper 121; ISBN 0 255 36522 5
£10.00

The Road to Serfdom

The Reader's Digest *condensed version*
Friedrich A. Hayek
Occasional Paper 122; ISBN 0 255 36530 6
£7.50

Bastiat's *The Law*

Introduction by Norman Barry
Occasional Paper 123; ISBN 0 255 36509 8
£7.50

A Globalist Manifesto for Public Policy

Charles Calomiris
Occasional Paper 124; ISBN 0 255 36525 X
£7.50

Euthanasia for Death Duties

Putting Inheritance Tax Out of Its Misery
Barry Bracewell-Milnes
Research Monograph 54; ISBN 0 255 36513 6
£10.00

Liberating the Land

The Case for Private Land-use Planning
Mark Pennington
Hobart Paper 143; ISBN 0 255 36508 X
£10.00

IEA Yearbook of Government Performance 2002/ 2003

Edited by Peter Warburton
Yearbook 1; ISBN 0 255 36532 2
£15.00

Britain's Relative Economic Performance, 1870– 1999

Nicholas Crafts
Research Monograph 55; ISBN 0 255 36524 1
£10.00

Should We Have Faith in Central Banks?

Otmar Issing
Occasional Paper 125; ISBN 0 255 36528 4
£7.50

The Dilemma of Democracy

Arthur Seldon

Hobart Paper 136 (reissue); ISBN 0 255 36536 5

£10.00

Capital Controls: a 'Cure' Worse Than the Problem?

Forrest Capie

Research Monograph 56; ISBN 0 255 36506 3

£10.00

The Poverty of 'Development Economics'

Deepak Lal

Hobart Paper 144 (reissue); ISBN 0 255 36519 5

£15.00

Should Britain Join the Euro?

The Chancellor's Five Tests Examined

Patrick Minford

Occasional Paper 126; ISBN 0 255 36527 6

£7.50

Post-Communist Transition: Some Lessons

Leszek Balcerowicz

Occasional Paper 127; ISBN 0 255 36533 0

£7.50

A Tribute to Peter Bauer

John Blundell et al.
Occasional Paper 128; ISBN 0 255 36531 4
£10.00

Employment Tribunals

Their Growth and the Case for Radical Reform
J. R. Shackleton
Hobart Paper 145; ISBN 0 255 36515 2
£10.00

Fifty Economic Fallacies Exposed

Geoffrey E. Wood
Occasional Paper 129; ISBN 0 255 36518 7
£12.50

A Market in Airport Slots

Keith Boyfield (editor), David Starkie, Tom Bass & Barry Humphreys
Readings 56; ISBN 0 255 36505 5
£10.00

Money, Inflation and the Constitutional Position of the Central Bank

Milton Friedman & Charles A. E. Goodhart
Readings 57; ISBN 0 255 36538 1
£10.00

Railway.com

Parallels between the early British railways and the ICT revolution

Robert C. B. Miller

Research Monograph 57; ISBN 0 255 36534 9

£12.50

To order copies of currently available IEA papers, or to enquire about availability, please contact:

Lavis Marketing
IEA orders
FREEPOST LON21280
Oxford OX3 7BR

Tel: 01865 767575
Fax: 01865 750079
Email: orders@lavismarketing.co.uk

The IEA also offers a subscription service to its publications. For a single annual payment, currently £40.00 in the UK, you will receive every title the IEA publishes across the course of a year, invitations to events, and discounts on our extensive back catalogue. For more information, please contact:

Subscriptions
The Institute of Economic Affairs
2 Lord North Street
London SW1P 3LB

Tel: 020 7799 8900
Fax: 020 7799 2137
Website: www.iea.org.uk